Tarot
INTERACTIONS

About the Author

Deborah Lipp began her study of the tarot in 1981, reads profession-ally, and has taught on the subject since 1993. She is the author of several popular books on occult topics, including *The Elements of Ritual, The Way of Four,* and *Merry Meet Again.* She has appeared in publications as diverse as *Llewellyn's Magical Almanac, PanGaia, Green Egg,* and *Mothering.* Deborah also writes on pop-culture topics and is the co-owner and chief writer at Basket of Kisses, a television and media blog. She has appeared in Indiewire, the *New York Times,* and elsewhere on topics such as *Mad Men* and James Bond. In addition, she holds a day job in the software industry.

Deborah lives just outside New York City with her spouse, Melissa, and an assortment of cats. She is the proud mother of Arthur Lipp-Bonewits, himself a skilled professional tarot reader. She's happy to say she gave him his first deck. Deborah is obsessed with logic puzzles, James Bond, and old musicals.

BECOME MORE INTUITIVE,
PSYCHIC & SKILLED AT READING CARDS

Tarot
INTERACTIONS

DEBORAH LIPP

Llewellyn Publications
Woodbury, Minnesota

First Edition
First Printing, 2015

Cover design by Ellen Lawson
Cover illustration by Elisabeth Alba
Editing by Andrea Neff
Illustrations on pages 94–95, 121–122 by Elisabeth Alba

For a full list of tarot art credits, please see page 251.

Llewellyn Publications is a registered trademark of Llewellyn Worldwide Ltd.

Library of Congress Cataloging-in-Publication Data
Lipp, Deborah, 1961–
  Tarot interactions : become more intuitive, psychic, and skilled at reading cards / by Deborah Lipp.—First Edition.
     pages cm
  Includes bibliographical references.
  ISBN 978-0-7387-4520-6
1. Tarot. I. Title.
  BF1879.T2L57 2015
  133.3'2424—dc23
                              2015012048

Llewellyn Worldwide Ltd. does not participate in, endorse, or have any authority or responsibility concerning private business transactions between our authors and the public.
  All mail addressed to the author is forwarded but the publisher cannot, unless specifically instructed by the author, give out an address or phone number.
  Any Internet references contained in this work are current at publication time, but the publisher cannot guarantee that a specific location will continue to be maintained. Please refer to the publisher's website for links to authors' websites and other sources.

Llewellyn Publications
A Division of Llewellyn Worldwide Ltd.
2143 Wooddale Drive
Woodbury, MN 55125-2989
www.llewellyn.com

Printed in the United States of America

Other Books by Deborah Lipp

The Elements of Ritual:
Air, Fire, Water & Earth in the Wiccan Circle
(Llewellyn, 2003)

The Way of Four:
Create Elemental Balance in Your Life
(Llewellyn, 2004)

The Way of Four Spellbook:
Working Magic with the Elements
(Llewellyn, 2006)

Merry Meet Again:
Lessons, Life & Love on the Path of a Wiccan High Priestess
(Llewellyn, 2013)

To Melissa Payne
Thank you for changing my life.

Thanks and Acknowledgments

Thanks first to my parents, and my paternal grandparents, who played endless games with me and taught me that cards feel good in my hands.

Thanks to Susan, my first tarot teacher, and Lorraine, another gifted teacher.

Thanks to every tarot reader with whom I've ever had an in-depth or ever-so-brief discussion about the cards. You've all made a difference. I'm afraid to name names here, because I know I've forgotten bunches of them, but I can at least mention Isaac Bonewits, Arthur Lipp-Bonewits, Nybor, Robin Wood, and Tzipora Katz. My tarot students have made a difference as well, including William Seligman, Orien LaPlante, and Barbara Giacalone.

Thanks to Eden Gray, my companion all these years.

Thanks to my tarot clients who allowed their readings to be used in this book. You are anonymous but not forgotten.

A huge thank you to my editor, Elysia Gallo, who made this a much better book despite my best efforts to stop her.

Contents

Illustrations and Chart

Introduction

I met my friend Susan in 1982. At that time, my life was rather dramatically in flux. I had just left my first husband, moved in with my mom, and changed jobs. I was twenty-one years old and it seemed like I'd already lived a lifetime.

When we first met, Susan pulled out her tarot cards and gave me a reading. I had questions about my ex-husband, and we identified one of the cards in the reading as him. She then took this card, moved it to the center of the layout, shuffled the rest of the cards, and did another reading—on him. Then she handed me the deck and said, "Now you read me." I'd never read before, but I was aided by the fact that this was Aleister Crowley's Thoth deck, and almost every card has a keyword of some kind on it. While most decks give you the names of the majors (Death, the Sun, and so on), this one labels (for example) the Two of Swords as Peace, the Five of Cups as Disappointment, and the Six of Wands as Victory. It was a little like having a cheat sheet, and I dove right in. Thus a lifetime of tarot reading began.

I come from a card-playing family. We started with all the little-kid games—Go Fish, War, Michigan Rummy—but quickly progressed to more interesting fare like Hearts, Gin Rummy, Oh Hell, and Double

Solitaire. Cards feel natural in my hands, and shuffling relaxes me. As soon as I touched the tarot cards, I knew these were for me.

I didn't stick with the Thoth deck. I admired Lady Frieda Harris's artwork more than I loved it, and the sense of chaotic movement in the cards didn't appeal to me. I acquired a Rider-Waite deck (often known today as Waite-Smith, the most popular deck in the world) and a secondhand copy of *Mastering the Tarot* (1973) by Eden Gray, a book I still recommend.

My first goal was to get "off book," as they say in theater. I worked daily to memorize the card meanings, flipping through the deck like flashcards until I had a few words for each card, both upright and reversed. *Mastering the Tarot* is an ideal book for this purpose, giving pithy, concise, yet deep meanings.

While memorizing, I was also reading the cards, first by flipping through the book for the meaning of every card, then by checking the book only when I got stuck. I read for myself and my sister, who was seventeen and game, and for any friends who were interested. Susan and I continued to read for each other, and I continued to learn from her and study on my own. By the time I was twenty-five, I was reading professionally, and I've done so ever since. I taught my first class in tarot around 1993, and some of my former students are today professional readers.

At some point in the mid-1990s, my then-husband, Isaac Bonewits, started insisting that I write a book on the tarot. He was a skilled reader and had even designed his own deck. He admired my ability and thought I had something important to say on the subject. We were already divorced by the time I published my first book (*The Elements of Ritual*, 2003), but Isaac never dropped the matter of a tarot book. He really wanted me to write one, and so, at last, I am doing so. Sadly, Isaac died in 2010. Nonetheless, I somehow feel his approval as I write.

This book isn't a "system." I haven't studied a system. I've read a number of books on tarot—I have a pretty decent library—and I've spent time with other tarot readers, both formally, in classes, and informally, just sharing knowledge and experience. What I'm teaching here is almost entirely my own; it's stuff I've learned by doing, concepts I've developed on my own, and my personal interpretation of the books I've read.

What Are Tarot Interactions?

I've coined the term "tarot interactions" to talk about different ways in which we can relate to, and use, tarot cards. Tarot isn't static; it interacts with its environment in a wide variety of ways. I started by thinking of various ways that cards relate to one another, and the way that various combinations of cards create unique wholes. You may think that there are 78 possible interpretations in a (78-card) deck, or perhaps 156, counting reversals. But when you consider that each two-card combination creates a unique and individual meaning, the number approaches 25,000, and when you also consider that every one of those 25,000 meanings changes based on its position in a reading, and a reading might have ten or more cards, we're already at the quarter-million mark, and we haven't even scratched the surface!

Cards interact with each other, with position, with the reader, and with the querent (the person receiving the reading). They interact with the context of the reading. You interact with the cards, with the querent, and with yourself as a reader. Understanding tarot interactions fundamentally changes your approach to tarot.

What Kinds of Cards Work with This Book?

Any. Most books on the tarot focus on a specific deck or a specific type of deck. A typical tarot book will be useful for any Waite-Smith–derived deck. However, *Tarot Interactions* applies to any tarot deck, and indeed, to any divinatory system using cards.

There are a lot of "oracle" decks out there, lovely decks of cards that do not correspond to the system known as tarot. They have different numbers of cards, different suits or no suits, and symbols that in no way are based on the medieval system known as tarot. Oracle decks may be based on Druid lore, or ogham (such as the Voice of the Trees deck), or on goddesses or crystals. They may simply be conceptual, or they may be based on an almost infinite number of other themes.

Throughout this book, I will use traditional tarot in my sample readings to illustrate my points. My personal interpretations are based on the Waite-Smith style of deck. However, the principles of interactive tarot apply to any kind of reading. Indeed, the principles in chapter 1 don't even require cards.

If you read using an alternative deck, you may find appendices A and B easily skipped: they are about meanings and patterns in Waite-Smith decks. However, the concept of meanings and patterns still matters to you! For example, chapter 3, which is about interacting with patterns, has material that doesn't apply to you, since it talks about suits and other traditional tarot symbols. But you can easily use those symbols as examples, and apply the underlying principles to your own preferred deck.

Who This Book Is For

By the time you read this, I expect that you'll have already done your flashcards. You know what the tarot is, what the major and minor arcana are, and what the suits are. You probably already own at least one deck, and have already begun reading with it.

If you're a beginner, that's fine. In fact, that's great. In that case, though, you will probably want some in-depth books on interpreting each card. As a teacher, I insist that all my tarot students go through the labor of memorization. It might not be fun, but there's no substitute for it. Yes, tarot is and should be intuitive, but starting from an underlying educational structure will improve your intuition, as we'll discuss in chapter 1. So while I hope to have your rapt attention in these pages, I do not want or expect to be your only resource. You can use the brief card interpretations I've provided in appendix A, but those almost certainly won't be enough. Purchase one or more "card-by-card" books, and study them. I provide recommendations at the end of this book.

But suppose you've already done all that. You know the cards pretty well, but you feel like you could go further with them. Perhaps you're doing great with the cards and you just want to dig deeper and read more. Or perhaps you feel like there's something lacking: a sense of freedom, a sense that the cards can be more than the sum of their parts.

Tarot Interactions is designed to take you from good to great, from understanding to experiencing. It is a tool you can use to stop *reading* the tarot and start *interacting* with it, or to read it not like a series of road signs, but like a story, or a poem, or the lyrics to a song. It is my hope and intention that this book will help you become more intuitive, more psychic, and more skilled in your approach to the cards. Do the homework and the exercises to enhance your experience. Keep the recommended journal. You'll be a very different reader at the end of this book than you are right now.

Let's begin.

ONE

Interaction with the Psyche

The first interaction we're going to discuss is the interaction with your inner self. We can call this your intuition, your deep mind, your Higher Self, or any number of other names. It's the interaction you use both first and last. For some people, becoming more in tune with this part of themselves is a struggle, and if that's true of you, you'll find every other section of this book to be more accessible than this one, because they don't deal with this area of struggle directly. But the whole time you're working with other tarot interactions, you're also working with yourself; you bring yourself to the table. So it makes sense to address this part of being a reader first.

Becoming Psychic

It would be gentler, at this moment, to refer to "becoming intuitive." "Psychic" is a hot-button word for many people. It feels weird, or spooky, or nonsensical. I use the word precisely because it *is* jarring, and that feeling, that discomfort, is exactly where most people's problem with releasing this ability lies.

Western culture treats psychic ability like a social faux pas. Partly this is because we are a rational culture that is primed to reject anything that seems irrational. People experience and believe in all sorts of "supernatural" things, but there's an attitude that you don't talk about it in polite company. However, I'd argue that this discomfort runs much deeper.

Propriety, in our culture, depends on keeping a certain amount of ourselves hidden. Just as we don't walk around naked in public, we don't reveal our psychological nakedness in public either. We keep up a facade. We are shielded, guarded, and private. This cultural norm varies from person to person, from region to region, from ethnicity to ethnicity, but in general, none of us are truly open except with those closest to us. It's obvious that any psychic ability, whether telepathy (knowing the thoughts of others) or empathy (knowing the feelings of others), would violate the social contract that we don't reveal our secrets in public. Thus, we have an unspoken agreement: *Don't show me yours, and I won't show you mine.*

Children don't have to be taught most social rules. Sure, we pull little fingers out of little noses and tell Junior not to do that in front of people, but for the most part, kids learn social structure by observation, not by instruction, and one observation that a child can easily make is that adults don't talk about one another's secrets, and don't even *know* them. Little Sally might get a timeout if she reveals something private about Aunt Margaret, and if she says she learned it by looking inside Aunt Margaret's head, she'll get a second punishment for being a liar. As we grow up understanding that being psychic is treated as a lie as well as rude, we suppress any psychic abilities.

But it goes even deeper. Remember: *Don't show me yours, and I won't show you mine.* As we grow, we develop our own secrets, our own pain and confusion and loss and longing that we don't want to share. We have unrequited crushes, dark dreams, untold rages, sexual fetishes, violent thoughts, and personal traumas. If we break the code—if we agree that inner secrets can be known, and this isn't a lie, and it isn't rude—

what's to stop others from breaking the code and knowing our own secrets? The social contract only works if everyone upholds it.

For all of these reasons, we have a strong incentive to reject the very notion of being psychic. When we *are* psychic, we usually use other words to describe it: a hunch, a feeling, intuition.

You see, this is why I'm using the rudest word: psychic. It begins the process of poking a hole into a social structure that holds back your abilities.

The Three Tools of Any Psychic Skill

There are a large number of mind skills. A few paragraphs ago, I defined telepathy as knowing the thoughts of others, and empathy as knowing the feelings of others. A third mind skill used by tarot readers is clairvoyance: knowing the future or the past. There are many other skills that don't concern us here. All mind skills rely on three tools: meditation, self-knowledge, and trust.

Meditation

Meditation is the first and most necessary step in developing any mind skill. It begins the process of giving you control over your mind, and also knowing its interior. Through meditation, you'll gain knowledge of how your thoughts behave, how they are when they're noisy, and how to go about quieting them. You'll learn the sound of your inner voice, which is so important, as, for many people, the "psychic voice" sounds different from the ordinary voice of day-to-day thoughts.

Many people find meditation frustrating and assume they're bad at it. It's important to recognize that "bad at it" is almost entirely a misconception! If part of the purpose of meditation is understanding how your mind behaves, then observing it *mis*behave is right on target. When your mind wanders during meditation, instead of thinking, "Crap, I suck at this," simply observe your mind wandering, and gently bring it back.

I liken this kind of meditation to what I do when I'm writing. I'm often distracted—by noises, by my spouse or my cat, by a game of solitaire—but ultimately I get back to writing. The distractions will happen, but I simply bring myself back to focus and continue writing. The measure of success is not "Did I experience distraction?" but "Did I write?"

Here's the thing, though. Suppose I get distracted by my adorable cat. Suppose I then start thinking things like, "Darn it! I shouldn't be distracted! What a dope I am to play with Callie instead of writing! I'm terrible at this!" Are those thoughts useful? Not really. You know what else those thoughts are not? They're not *writing*. Beating myself up about my distraction is *just another distraction*.

Meditation allows me to experience my inner voices, my noises, my distractions, my self-recriminations, and to gently overcome them. That doesn't mean they go away. I will continue to have stray thoughts when I meditate, just as I will continue to notice my cute cat. But as I learn to concentrate better, I can notice distractions without being *overcome* by them.

There are other parts of your mind besides a bunch of stray thoughts, and a meditation practice will allow those parts to come out. These include the psychic and intuitive parts.

There are a number of wonderful books to help you begin meditating. One of my favorites is *Meditation: The Complete Guide* (2011) by Patricia Monaghan and Eleanor Viereck. What's great about this book is that it introduces a wide variety of techniques.

There's no rule that meditation means "sitting with legs crossed, silencing the mind while reciting a mantra," yet that's what most people think. There are stillness meditations and chanting meditations, loving-kindness, zazen, walking, drumming, and many other varieties. Choose a technique that suits you, be kind to yourself when you struggle, and appreciate the journey without any preconceptions about the result.

I was first exposed to meditation in the 1970s, through friends who hung out at ashrams and were interested in Transcendental Meditation. Years later, my tarot teacher, Susan, gave me a set of written instructions for meditation. The instructions were simple: Start by picturing one thing, visualizing *anything* about it, for fifteen minutes. For example, if you visualize a tree, you can see, in your mind's eye, any tree, and you can picture it through the seasons. You can imagine details of its leaves and bark, and you can picture climbing it or picnicking under it. You can imagine its scent, and feel the breeze blowing through it. Your mind can wander at will, as long as it wanders in a treelike direction. Eliminate only those thoughts that are non-tree.

The instructions go on to say that only once you feel comfortable with this kind of visualization should you move on to concentrating on a single image of a tree and attempting to hold it throughout the meditation.

I began with fifteen-minute sessions at least three times a week, increasing to twenty minutes after a while. I also added other areas of concentration. For example, when driving, I would practice thinking only about driving. Again, I would allow myself to recall past drives, think about my car, and so on, eliminating only non-drive thoughts. Even when I had advanced to "picture only the tree" during private, at-home meditation, I continued using the looser, visualize-anything style while driving, walking, and doing housework.

This was very effective mind training. It improved my meditation and visualization skills, and also allowed me to get better at being in the moment.

After years of that practice, I eventually became less disciplined. Currently I aim for once a week, though I frequently do less and occasionally do more. This is above and beyond when I practice the simple meditation of deep breathing and visualization for a few moments prior to any occasion when mind skills are called upon (such as when doing a reading).

I do a seated meditation that combines a short prayer with breathing and mala (meditation) beads. I take a deep breath, release it, say the prayer, move to the next bead, and repeat. I love the way beads free me from counting or using a timer, and also give me something to touch while I focus my mind. In addition, I regularly meditate in a hot bath. The hot water is relaxing and mind-altering, and I use it to visualize cleansing and release from stray thoughts and concerns while clearing my mind.

I have been meditating for almost forty years, beginning in my teens. It amazes me that even though I still catch my mind wandering frequently, the meditation leaves me better able to focus, relax, and reach a deeper part of my mind.

Self-Knowledge

Part of self-knowledge will come from meditation. You'll learn the sound of your inner voice, your fears, your doubts, as they arise in the course of gaining more control over your own mind. But self-knowledge is more than that.

Remember the unspoken principle: *Don't show me yours, and I won't show you mine.* Part of what blocks your psychic talents (to the extent that they are blocked) is your willingness to uphold this bargain. You do this in part because you have inner doors that you don't wish to be opened.

When there are parts of yourself that cannot be released—parts you may not even know about—it means there are places in your psyche where you simply cannot go. Your subconscious will stop you cold.

I had a student who was invariably attacked during guided meditation. We'd be going on an inner journey, and regardless of the instruction, it would turn violent. I might say, "You meet a kind stranger who gives you a gift," and then ask the class, after the journey was over, to describe the stranger and the gift, and this one student would say, "The stranger strangled me and then shoved the gift down my throat." My student wasn't aware of how unusual—and upsetting—these incidents were, and had no conscious memory of violence in her past. Yet something was clearly wrong. We were unable to proceed with our meditation work until she did the psychological work necessary to free herself from these violent and violating images.

The more you know what your inner blocks are and how they affect you, the more you bring your shadow into light, where it can be examined and explored, the weaker will become your internal commitment to *Don't show me yours*.

Inner work can take myriad forms, from studying the work of self-help gurus, to attending workshops, to active imagination, inner-child work, addiction recovery, traditional therapy, and more. Don't assume you can explore every dark corner alone. Therapy made me a better psychic, and perhaps the same will be true for you. Certainly if you're like my student, and the inner blocks are violent and frightening, you'll do much better, and feel safer, with someone else's assistance.

Your psychic skills are only as free as you are. The freer you make yourself, in a psychological sense, the stronger your mind skills will be.

Trust

Imagine your psychic skills as a person residing deep inside you. As we've discussed, this person was once sent to hide. Perhaps she was berated, or called a liar, or called crazy. Perhaps anytime you've heard from her (hunches you've had, for example), you've said, "That's ridiculous." She's been hiding inside you for most of your life, scurrying away every time she's called "ridiculous."

Gently, you're going to coax her out. As with any frightened child, the way you're going to do this is by establishing trust. How?

Don't berate, criticize, or disbelieve her. Doing so drives her (or him—your inner child's gender generally matches your own) back inside.

What will happen is something like this: You're giving a reading, and you think to say something. You see the Justice card and you want to say, "This relates to a legal matter." That seems kind of bold, though, so instead you rattle off a list of potential meanings of the card, including "a legal matter." What you did was distrust the "Psychic Child," and now she has retreated and has nothing more to say to you.

Instead, if you say exactly what you think, the trusted Psychic Child might give you more information. The next thought that pops into your head might be "family court." Again, you could refrain from saying that, and the Psychic Child will feel distrusted and retreat, or you could take the risk and say it, and be rewarded with more and more information that is psychic and accurate.

I've experienced exactly this sort of cycle many, many times: trusting the inner voice and being rewarded with more information; distrusting the inner voice and feeling the source of knowledge dry up. I know many other readers who've experienced the same things. The power of trust applies broadly to almost any mind skill, from clairvoyance to automatic writing to lucid dreaming. *Trust the inner voice.*

Your querent may lie. People do it all the time. They may have secrets they're uncomfortable sharing, they may be testing you by purposely withholding information, or they may simply not be thinking of the scenario that validates what you've said. I'll give you an example. If you, as a psychic, told me that I had an Aunt Amelia, I'd tell you flat out that you were wrong. I had an Aunt Milly, known as "Mimi," but I actually had to look up her given name in order to write this paragraph. I'd have guessed that her full name was Millicent or Mildred; I didn't know it was Amelia, and I didn't know her as Milly when she was alive, just Mimi. Yet, if your Psychic Child told you that I had an Aunt Amelia, she would be right and I, the querent, would be wrong.

So your job as a psychic isn't to trust the querent. Your job is to trust yourself, trust the Psychic Child, trust the inner voice. The more trust you feed it, the more it will thrive.

How Tarot Helps in Interaction with the Psyche

The three tools I just described are essential for developing virtually any mind skill. When working to develop the specific psychic talents that will help you as a tarot reader, you can allow tarot itself to help you.

Memorization as Intermediary

As you work to memorize card meanings, you'll have a distraction from the self-doubt that accompanies psychic ability. Remember the Psychic Child—she shies away when treated with doubt. Yet we adults, raised in a culture that treats such knowledge as nonsense, cannot avoid having at least some small touch of doubt.

It helps, at first, to look at (for example) the Three of Swords and think, "Sorrow, heartbreak," and just say that, rather than trying to experience an intuitive sense of the card meaning in this reading of your own. The cards are, in this way, a conduit.

Lots of mind-training techniques involve an intermediary of some kind. Meditating on a mandala (a sacred geometric symbol) gives the mind something to latch on to during the process, and makes meditating easier than just sitting in "no thought." Similarly, lighting a candle allows you to focus your mind on a prayer. You *could* just pray, but many people light a candle, using the object (the light) and the ritual of lighting the way that a meditator uses a mandala.

Thinking of your book knowledge about tarot also helps you increase self-trust, which helps the Psychic Child emerge. *The card means* this *because* this *is the meaning I studied and memorized.* You are more likely to trust in learned meanings than in your own intuitive sense at first, but as long as there's self-trust, and you allow yourself to speak from a place of self-trust, your skills will improve.

Tarot Gets You Past Social Barriers

Using the cards (or indeed, any divination tool) allows you to bypass the issue of social propriety. In many readings, I've said, "It's not me saying this, it's the cards." I've even disagreed with the cards during a reading, but I still gave a standard interpretation of the card rather than my opinion. By assuring the querent that you're reading the cards and keeping your personal opinion out of it, you can avoid the discomfort of inappropriateness. You're not a clod saying the wrong thing, you're a reader giving professional counsel!

Like you, the querent is more likely to trust the cards, at first, than the person reading them. This allows you to tap into that trust to build up your own *self*-trust, and the Psychic Child within is paying attention to both. Having a querent trust you can be daunting, but it also gives you a boost that lets you move forward with a reading. Most querents will find the cards somewhat spooky or fascinating or spiritual. The social contract, now, is that the two of you are engaging with a spiritual tool, and this different social contract will assist in freeing your psychic talents.

Ancient Power of the Tarot

Tarot cards have been around for almost six hundred years. Many of the symbols they depict have been used by occultists for far longer. The meanings of sun, moon, rivers, paths, swords, dogs, clouds, and so on have an ancient and archetypal resonance.

Using the cards allows you to tap into these ancient repositories of meaning. You're drawing not just on the limited resources of one person (you), but on the vast resources of everyone who has read the tarot for hundreds of years, and of the collective unconsciousness's almost infinite knowledge of its symbols.

Memorized meanings, the use of an intermediary tool, shifting the social contract, and tapping into ancient wisdom are all means by which the tarot allows you to improve your own psychic talents.

Three Phases to Becoming a More Psychic Reader

Now let's look at how you can use a three-phase approach to become more psychic in your interactions with the tarot. These phases assume you're also doing the work necessary to develop your abilities with the three tools of any mind skill: meditation, self-knowledge, and trust.

Phase One: Let Go and Let Cards

Phase one is where you let the cards do the talking. Don't try to determine if you're psychic or intuitive or kidding yourself or what. Just read the cards. Work with memorized meanings, and read what you see before you.

It's absolutely fine during this phase to study the little booklet that comes with any tarot deck. Those meanings are generally incredibly limited, and you'll want to expand out from there, but the booklet will give you very short keywords that are easy to commit to memory. You can also use the short card meanings in appendix A of this book, and delve into the recommended reading in appendix C.

Get off-book as soon as you can, but don't worry about "reading" anything except the meanings and positions of cards (we'll get to that soon).

Phase one is all about using the power of the tarot to help you in your quest to improve your mind skills. It's about letting the Psychic Child feel it's safe to come out.

Phase Two: Interact with the Cards

Here, reader, is where the fun begins.

Simply start by asking yourself, *What do I see?* I'll give you a hint: you've been in phase two all along. How? Well, as you've been memorizing, you've been remembering selectively. Memory, after all, is not perfect. You'll remember some meanings more clearly than others, and once you're off-book, those meanings might even develop subtle distortions. They will start to match up with the cards as you perceive them.

It's going to be tremendously important, at this stage, to pick a deck you really like. Most tarot readers have several decks of cards, if not dozens, but most of us read with just one or a few. I'll switch decks if I feel stuck, and if I'm feeling particularly "head blind" (not at all psychic), I'll go back to the deck I learned on as a kind of renewal. Despite switching around, almost every reading I do lately is with the Robin Wood Tarot (illustration 1). Other decks I've read with in heavy rotation include the Rider-Waite, Hanson-Roberts, and Sacred Rose.

Robin Wood Tarot

Gilded Tarot

Universal Tarot

Medieval Tarot

Illustration 1: The Magician Card in a Variety of Tarot Decks

The point is that, if the deck is something you interact with, you should feel like that's possible. Isaac Bonewits used to say, "Choose the deck you think is prettiest," but "pretty" is a loaded word and may not be a word that works for you. Instead, choose a deck that you feel connected to, that resonates with you, that feels like yours. Do the illustrations make you snicker? Wrong deck. Are the cards laden with symbols that confuse you? Wrong deck. Conversely, does a lack of symbols feel like freefall, like there's nothing to latch on to? Wrong deck. With the wealth of decks available on the market, it shouldn't be hard to find a deck you can connect to, and if you switch to a different one at some point in the future, that's fine too.

When interacting with the cards, the first question is *What do you see?*

Illustration 2: Queen of Pentacles (Universal Tarot)

What do you see in the Queen of Pentacles (illustration 2)? Close your eyes for a moment, take a deep breath, and relax. (Do you see how meditation will help you as a reader? Quick access to a relaxed state is a big plus!) Open your eyes and allow them to scan lightly over the card. What do you see? Has your eye noticed the downcast gaze of the queen, looking at what she holds and not at the greenery around her? Have you taken in the mountains in the background? The bulls on her throne?

You're going to scan this way multiple times. You'll start by doing it as you study the cards. Some of it may be subconscious; you won't even realize the way that your observation of a card affects the way you remember its meaning. Our old friend *Mastering the Tarot* (by Eden Gray) refers to the Queen of Pentacles as a woman who is intelligent, creative, good in business, good with gardens and children, and sometimes "melancholy and moody." If you're struck by the lush garden in the card, you're likely to remember her creative, fertile, and productive aspects. If you focus on the bulls, you might think she's "bullish" and recall that she's good with money. (You might even remember that bulls are associated with an upswing in the stock market!) Or you might notice her downward gaze, in which case you're more likely to recall "melancholy and moody."

Some people find that scanning a card this way is enhanced by using a deck with lots of imagery, so that the eye may fall on any of the many details of a card. Others find that their mind's eye fills in the details best with a card that is more sparsely illustrated. Similarly, your eye may find images better if the illustrations are realistic, or fanciful, or primitive, or if they're colorful, or black and white. Everyone is different. Spend time with different imagery and see what works for you (illustration 3).

Illustration 3: Two Queens:
The Anna.K Tarot (left) has a simple Queen of Swords, while the
Tarot Illuminati (right) has a highly detailed Queen of Swords

Remember, we're still studying; we haven't gotten to a reading yet.

Think about actors. More than one film director has said that the most important decision is casting. The actor transforms the role, brings it to life, and finds nuances and meaning that didn't seem to be in the script, often without deviating from the written page. Sure, sometimes actors improvise, but this interpretation and enlivening happens even when every word is kept intact, even when it's Shakespeare or some other author whose words are never tampered with.

Like an actor, you're taking the script (the interpretation of the cards that you're studying) and breathing life into it simply by interacting with it. The actor reads, studies, imagines, and thinks about the script. You read, study, imagine, gaze at, and observe the cards.

An actor might do research. Actors might spend a day with police, with prisoners, with doctors, to try to deepen their knowledge of what it is to be those people. Tarot readers also do research, studying different books about the tarot, exploring different decks, taking classes, and chatting with other readers.

Finally, an actor gets to perform, on stage or before a camera. At this point, there's a great deal more interaction, because there are other actors. There's also the opportunity to try out different line readings: "I love you" is different as a whisper or a shout, or with a question mark at the end.

Your "performance day" is the reading. Your co-star is the querent, and your line readings are what you notice in the cards *in that moment*.

You've memorized the Queen of Pentacles and recall that she is fertile, good in business, or melancholy. Yet when the cards are before you, your eye notices the bull again and again. You decide to stick with the business interpretation and set aside the other meanings.

Your querent will respond better to "good in business" than to "maybe good in business, maybe a good mother, maybe a gardener." Remember, the trust that you build with the querent is an energy you can tap into to help yourself become more psychic, and the Psychic Child will respond to that trust as well.

There's another level of interacting with what you see, and that is seeing things that are uniquely your own.

To me, the Four of Wands always looks like a wedding (illustration 4). This is not an interpretation that you'll find in books on the tarot written before the 1960s, but I'm not the only one who sees it that way, and this meaning appears in newer books. You'll find, for example, that Robin Wood (*Robin Wood Tarot: The Book*, 1998) says the meaning of this card is "harmony, romance, a wedding." The meaning comes from looking: it *looks like* a wedding, and so it *became* a wedding to many tarot readers. In other words, the meaning is based on interacting with the card.

Illustration 4: Four of Wands
(Universal Tarot)

Your interactions with the cards can transcend preferring one by-the-book meaning over another. You might see something in a card that a teacher hasn't told you is there. If you see it, allow for the possibility that the card is showing it to you, that it's interacting with you. (I'm not suggesting that cards are sentient beings, but this metaphor is the simplest way to describe the experience.)

Phase Three: Interact with Your Voice

This is the part of becoming psychic that involves trust, and releasing the Psychic Child. You've looked at the Queen of Pentacles and said, "Good in business." By saying that, you've opened a door.

Now listen to your voice saying that, and see if there's more to say. Sometimes, when we say something definitively, it unlocks a second statement, and perhaps a third after that.

If you'd said, "Maybe business, maybe gardening," that might have been a moment to discover that the next words out of your mouth were, "No, definitely business." On the other hand, if you were *thinking* "business" but hedged your bets with the "maybe," you might have frightened off the Psychic Child. You see, the key to this phase of interacting with your voice is never hedge. If you have the thought, speak the thought. That doesn't mean you have to be certain of everything you say, and it definitely doesn't mean you should pretend to be certain when you're not. It means to speak the words your inner voice is saying. Often, we have an inner dialogue that sounds like this:

> *Inner Voice:* That Queen of Pentacles ... good in business.
>
> *Rational Mind:* I can't possibly know that. I should say "maybe."
>
> *Inner Voice:* Fine, ignore me. I'll just go sit in the corner.

Speaking the words of the inner voice is what's crucial here. Sometimes the inner voice itself will say "maybe," and that's fine.

I find it's often easier to look straight at the cards when I'm speaking these thoughts. Eye contact with a querent is going to get me thinking about her, about how she's reacting, and about whether I'm being offensive to her. This is a card-based interaction, and looking at the card helps. Ultimately you want to be able to look at the querent, of course, but when I find that my flow of words feels interrupted, I look down at the cards before me and speak my words directly from the images that inspire them.

Suppose you didn't reject a thought and went straight to "business," or got to "business" with your "maybe," which was all you had in that moment. Now there might be more words. You might be able to describe the specific business, or the specific job within the field of business, going from "good with business" to "someone like an accountant or finance person." Speaking from a place of confidence and intuition opens up more words. And speaking *those* words can open still more words.

This process will get easier with multiple cards, and chapters 3 through 6 will give lots of examples of multi-card interactions that will allow your interaction with your own psyche to flourish. It took me years of reading tarot before I was really good, and really psychic, with a single-card reading.

Notice how interacting with the cards through words has its own phases: first through standard card interpretations, then through riffs on those interpretations, and finally, through spontaneous interaction with your words alone.

A beginner can always rely on an outward flow, from standard interpretations into a larger understanding. Indeed, after reading for more than thirty years, I still often go back to that. It's a good place from which to find one's voice, to clear the psychic throat.

But you can also push yourself out, away from the cards, into really flying with your voice. Ultimately, you can speak straight from a deeply intuitive place, as if the cards aren't even there. A "cold reading" is a reading without any divinatory tool (cards, stones, tea leaves, etc.). There are times when you can read as if "cold," except the cards are present. This intuitive speaking can be challenging but also rewarding, and if there are times when building from the basics outward doesn't seem to be working, an "almost cold" technique can be an effective way to shake things up and get the psychic juices flowing.

Speed

This technique pushes you to reach a different part of yourself. Because you are laying out cards very fast, you have no time to think. With this technique, you can't study the cards or try to remember what they mean. This pushes the Psychic Child to come to the forefront, taking over from logic and reason, because there is no time for logic or reason.

To use speed to train your psychic skills, you should be grounded and centered. Before you start, take a few deep, cleansing breaths. Then begin by sitting down with a querent. When you're experimenting, querents can often be friends and family. This technique does work alone, but the discipline of moving rapidly is enhanced by having someone else there to impel you forward.

The querent asks a question, then you lay down the first card and say immediately what you see. The minute you begin to hesitate, drop the next card directly on top of it—and then the next, and the next.

Here's a sample reading I did to get a quick snapshot of a friend's relationship problems (illustration 5). The entire thing, from beginning to end, took one minute, during which I recorded myself speaking.

Six of Wands: Victory experienced. Starting something great, and that was beautiful, and uh…

The Moon in reverse: It's really hard to understand what's going on right now, and uh, howling doesn't help…

Ace of Wands: Very phallic, time to start over, very sexual, sexually related, um…

Ten of Wands: Carrying the burden all yourself, yeah, this is accurate to the question, uh…

Five of Swords: Being a little sneaky with the victory, laughing, um, being apart, uh…

Queen of Pentacles: Um, a loving and kind and fertile solution, fertile outcome. Okay, this feels like an outcome card. I'm going to stop.

Moon reversed   *Ten of Wands*   *Queen of Pentacles*

Six of Wands   *Ace of Wands*   *Five of Swords*

Illustration 5: Speed Reading (Robin Wood Tarot)

Notice that I moved as quickly as possible. When I found myself saying "uh" or "um," I laid down the next card. I said everything out loud, including the idea that this was accurate; in this way, I kept the words flowing and affirmed to myself what I was seeing. I slowed down a little at the Five of Swords (a card that often slows me down), caught myself, and quickly laid down the next card. As you can see, just six cards at about ten seconds per card can give an accurate assessment of a relationship, which was confirmed by the querent. (This couple is doing fine and they are basically happy, but they were going through a rough patch that was affecting their sex life and making the querent feel lonely.)

Confusion

Planned confusion can be another way of bypassing the rational mind. I'm going to explain this by telling a story.

I fell in love with the Tarot Art Nouveau the first time I saw it (illustration 6). It's simply beautiful, and I've been a little obsessed with Art Nouveau since I was a teenager. I purchased the deck but found it difficult to use. Because every card has an illustration on it, I didn't realize that the Tarot Art Nouveau is practically a "pip" deck. A pip deck is a deck in which the major arcana have images, but the minor arcana just have pips (symbols of the suit), like ordinary playing cards, so that the Four of Wands has no image besides four wands.

The Tarot Art Nouveau deck actually does have an image on every card, but there's a sameness to them that makes them difficult to read. Facial expressions and body language convey meaning, but it's far too subtle for me. The minors, for me, are almost unreadable; I have to rely on my memory of what cards mean, essentially visualizing other decks' versions of a card. The fact that the main labels on the cards are in Spanish (*bastoni* for wands, *espadas* for swords) makes that harder. This deck, beautiful as it is, is almost impossible for me to connect to, and even the majors feel distant.

So there I was, giving a reading with my new deck, and feeling lost. I got a kind of floaty feeling in my head, like I didn't know what I was saying. Having spent years training myself to interact with my voice and release my Psychic Child, I just kept talking. The whole time, I felt confused, and fluttery, and a little anxious. When I was done, I felt exhausted. At the same time, it was one of the most psychic readings I'd ever given, and the querent was amazed.

Illustration 6: Tarot Art Nouveau

My son was around when I gave that reading, and felt that the psychic experience was caused by my confusion. Because I had no rational way of connecting to the deck, I got pushed into an irrational and intuitive mindset. On subsequent occasions, he would suggest that I use that deck and would often request it if I was reading for him. Sometimes I would agree, and always with the same result—a floaty, almost panicked feeling, and astonishingly accurate content for the querent.

I rarely use that deck anymore. I like the result, but I dislike the feeling of achieving it. However, I encourage any reader to try the same experiment. Work with a deck that feels too blank (if you like a lot of detail) or too crowded (if you like a sparser look). Work with a deck that feels outside your comfort zone. Note not just your feelings but also your results.

Exercises

Exercise 1: Meditation

Most people who begin a meditation practice try one method and stick with it. Perhaps you already have a practice that works for you, but perhaps you have only ever used one method, or you do not meditate at all.

Try at least one method of meditation that is new to you. Use this method at least twice a week for at least a month.

EXAMPLES:

- Walking meditation
- Drumming
- Buddhist loving-kindness meditation
- Candle-gazing
- Use of a prayer or mantra

Exercise 2: Journal

Begin keeping a journal of your tarot readings. Note the date, the deck used, the querent's question (if any), and the cards. You can also note how things turned out, if possible.

Throughout the rest of this book, you'll be asked to write the results of various exercises in this journal.

Exercise 3: Speed Reading

Do this exercise with a companion as your querent. If you must work alone, speak out loud, as if to a querent. You can record your voice for noting in your journal later.

1. Take a series of deep, calming breaths. Make sure you feel centered before you begin.

2. Shuffle or mix your cards, and allow the process of shuffling to continue centering you.[1]

3. Lay down the first card and immediately begin speaking. Don't let yourself pause for a breath. Say whatever comes to mind, whatever you remember about the card. Spend no more than ten to fifteen seconds on the card.

4. Lay down the next card on top of, or next to, the first card. Remember, *don't stop to think*, just keep talking.

5. After you have laid down five to seven cards, put the deck down.

6. Ask your querent what worked and what didn't. Make notes in your journal.

7. Repeat this exercise several times. Use it anytime you feel psychically clogged up to reconnect to a sense of spontaneity.

---

1. Throughout this book, I'll instruct you to "shuffle." Many people don't know how to shuffle cards, or feel uncomfortable doing so. Wherever you see this instruction, please read it to mean "shuffle or mix as you prefer."

TWO

Interaction
with Other Disciplines

The tarot can interact with a number of other disciplines. The very nature of painting images onto cards has a plasticity that allows it to become what you, the reader, need it to be. In the previous chapter, we discussed the way in which your personal taste should determine the deck(s) you use. But it's not just a matter of taste. Combining tarot with other interests and areas of expertise allows the tarot to interact with your own knowledge, for fascinating results!

Sometimes this kind of interaction can be reciprocal: the other discipline can augment a card reading, and a card reading can also enhance the other discipline. Other times, it's simply a matter of augmenting tarot with prior knowledge or experience. Often, choosing a deck that matches that prior knowledge or experience enhances and deepens the experience of using the cards.

Esoteric Disciplines

Many people who are interested in esoteric arts such as tarot are interested in several. You may already be adept at astrology, numerology, or

Kabbalah. Or you may have expertise in herbalism, or perhaps in the properties of crystals.

Kabbalah

Modern tarot came to be as a result of the highly influential deck created by Arthur Edward Waite and Pamela Colman Smith. This deck, known as the Rider-Waite or the Waite-Smith, was first published in 1909. The Waite-Smith deck was the first to illustrate all 78 cards; older decks (dating back to about 1440) were always what I call pip decks, with only the majors fully illustrated. Waite-Smith is the most popular and influential tarot deck in the world, with many, many decks based directly on it.

Members of the Hermetic Order of the Golden Dawn, Waite and Smith created a deck based on their esoteric studies. The Golden Dawn saw the tarot as Kabbalistic. Just as the Kabbalah has ten sephiroth (each with four emanations) and twenty-two paths, the tarot has twenty-two major arcana, and the minors consist of four suits, each with ten numbered cards and four court cards.

Illustration 7: Kabbalistic Symbolism
in the Tarot (Classic Tarot)

So the first esoteric discipline that can interact with the tarot is Kabbalah. If you study Kabbalah, you will find many decks with Kabbalistic elements that will enhance your understanding of the cards, starting with Waite-Smith, Classic, Universal, and Thoth. An excellent choice is the Witches Tarot by Ellen Cannon Reed, because she designed the deck to be accessible to beginning students of Kabbalah.

Using a deck with Kabbalistic symbols or meanings is one interaction: the Kabbalah interacts with tarot (illustration 7). But you can also reverse that and have tarot interact with Kabbalah, particularly Kabbalah as studied in the Western mystery traditions.

"Pathworking" is a technique whereby you astrally travel one of the paths of the Tree of Life. This seems to have arisen with the Golden Dawn or one of its early offshoots. Many volumes have been written on the subject,[2] and many courses and guided journeys are available. Tarot has often been used in conjunction with pathworking. Each card of the major arcana is considered to correspond to one of the paths, and decks have been designed specifically so that meditating on the correct card facilitates journeying on the corresponding path. This meditation is one way for the tarot to interact with Kabbalistic work. However, you could get more creative or intuitive with that.

Shuffle the cards and draw one for your pathworking, perhaps laying it on top of an image of the Tree of Life, placing it on the path you're focused on. Or place the designated card on the path, then shuffle and lay a second card beside it. Use the randomly selected card as part of the meditation or as a divinatory guide, letting you know where the pathworking will take you.

Astrology

If you study astrology, you'll find many decks that will interact with that art. The Thoth deck shows a planet in a sign on almost every card. This

---

2. *Magical Pathworking: Techniques of Active Imagination* by Nick Farrell (Llewellyn, 2004) and *The Initiate's Book of Pathworkings: A Bridge of Dreams* by Dolores Ashcroft-Nowicki (Red Wheel/Weiser, 1999), to name two.

gives you more to read, more to speak from, more to riff on, and deepens your knowledge of the card if you're an astrologer. Among many other astrological choices are the Elemental Tarot and the Zodiac Tarot.

An astrologer can also use tarot to enhance chart reading. Shuffle the cards and lay one on a particular planet in a chart to deepen your interpretation. You can place a card on each house or on each significant transit while creating a chart interpretation. For a professional astrologer, this can be a powerful addition when sitting with an astrology client for a reading. Looking at a difficult aspect of a chart, you can lay a card on it to suggest a current course of action.

I'm friends with an astrologer with whom I sometimes trade readings; that is, she does my chart and I read her cards. Her feeling is that, while astrology is an amazing tool for understanding a year or a lifetime, she prefers tarot for here, today. She finds it useful for answering the question "What do I do now?" With that in mind, an astrologer can consider how two readings can overlap, using astrology for the long term and overlaying that with practical, tarot-based advice for the short term.

Other Esoteric Arts

If you study numerology, virtually any tarot deck can interact with that discipline, since almost every deck has numbered cards. Of course, there are multiple kinds of numerology. A Kabbalistic tarot deck will use Kabbalistic numerology, and you should be aware of that if you use a different system.

You can find a tarot deck on the market that ties into almost any esoteric art, and this will help you combine your interests in a way that enhances each. The Crystal Tarot, the Herbal Tarot, and the Tree Tarot (Das Baum Tarot) are a few examples.

Cultural Disciplines

There are innumerable tarot decks based on specific pantheons, mythologies, cultural traditions, and folklore, and there are also cross-cultural mythic decks (often with a goddess theme). There are far too many to list more than a few here, although examples include Norse, Yoruban, Greek, Arthurian, and Druidic. There are also location-specific decks, like the Tarot of Prague, and decks based on specific religious traditions, including Christian, Hindu, Wiccan, Buddhist, and Jewish.

You might choose one of these decks because the cultural resonances allow you to connect to the cards at a deeper level. You might do so because adding a spiritual component to your readings feels right to you, and enhances the sense of import you bring to your use of the cards. You might also choose such a deck because the idea of storytelling as connected to the cards makes sense to you: the cards tell a story, so a story-based deck helps you move through tarot narratives. (Chapter 6 will have more about story and its relation to the cards.)

Just as these traditions interact with the cards, so can you use the cards to interact with the traditions. For example, if you work with spirit guides or angels, a deck that corresponds to the work you do can help guide you. Pick one or several cards to indicate where messages might be coming from, or to suggest a fruitful area for meditation or prayer.

Other Disciplines

By now, if you didn't know it before, you can see that tarot can interact with a wide range of personal interests. Importantly for our purposes, this interaction can empower you as a reader. If you're a beginner at tarot but an expert in some other area, the confidence you derive from your expertise can help boost your tarot skills. The feeling of connection that you have with your area of expertise or interest will increase your connection to the tarot. The comfort we sometimes have with our hobbies or interests—that "this is my place" feeling—can make us more comfortable with our cards, and comfort is something that brings the Psychic Child out to play.

Suppose, though, that the tarot is your first foray into esotericism, and you're not all that interested in mythology or folklore. You still have plenty of options for decks that might give you the kind of interaction we're talking about.

There are fantasy, fairy, and Steampunk decks. If literature is your thing, a Shakespeare, Tolkien, Jane Austen, Wonderland, or Lovecraft deck might be a compelling choice. If you're interested in fine art, an Art Nouveau, Bosch, da Vinci, or Dali deck might inspire you. There are decks for historians and scientists, and there's a Jungian Tarot if psychology fascinates you.

There are also decks that could simply suit your life. An LGBT, African-American, or teen deck might feel more "you," and a humorous or parody deck might click with that side of your personality.

Tarot can interact with any of these disciplines or interests. Again, when used with a simple shuffle-and-draw technique, tarot cards that resonate with work you're doing can suggest plot twists in your writing, areas of study for research projects, or interpretations of dreams. Indeed, tarot can interact with all areas of life. This chapter simply suggests ways in which disciplines, arts, and work you might have thought entirely separate from the tarot can become part of a greater whole.

Exercises

The following three pathworking exercises should be done in conjunction with a deep study of Kabbalah and pathworking. They are not meant as a replacement for either. Use your own studies in Kabbalah to guide your process through the following steps.

Pathworking Exercise 1
Have a picture of the Tree of Life available.

1. Separate a deck so that you are working only with the major arcana. If you do this exercise on a regular basis, consider purchasing one of the many decks that has only majors.

2. Place the cards in order, beginning with the Fool and ending with the World.

3. Center yourself using deep, cleansing breaths.

4. Lay the first card (the Fool) down before you. If your picture of the Tree of Life is large enough, lay the card directly on the path from Kether to Chokmah, often called path 0 because of its correspondence to the Fool.

5. Visualize yourself as being inside the card. You *are* the Fool. Visualize yourself actually walking the path from Kether (Crown) to Chokmah (Wisdom).

6. Now is the time to meditate on this path. You're moving from the Crown to Wisdom. You are the Fool. What does it mean to be a Fool and move to Wisdom?

7. When you're finished, visualize yourself reentering your physical body. Reconnect to the earth. Have a light snack.

8. Move the Fool to the bottom of your ordered majors.

9. Repeat this exercise weekly for twenty-two weeks, using a different card and path each week.

Pathworking Exercise 2

This exercise is for the advanced student of the Kabbalah who has already worked with paths and wants to explore in a different way.

1. Work with the same deck as in the previous exercise, but this time shuffle the majors.

2. Center yourself using deep, cleansing breaths.

3. Place a single card before you. This card determines the path you will walk.

4. Do steps 5 through 7 from the previous exercise for the path you have selected.

Pathworking Exercise 3

This exercise is also for advanced students of the Kabbalah and offers a completely different perspective on pathworking. For this exercise, you will need a large image of the Tree of Life so that you can lay cards on the path, or you can choose a path mentally. As with Pathworking Exercise 1, you can repeat this exercise weekly for twenty-two weeks.

1. Work with the same deck as in the previous exercises, and shuffle the majors.

2. Center yourself using deep, cleansing breaths.

3. Place a single card on the first path, or simply hold the mental image that it is on the first path. The card you have selected should not change the path you have chosen to walk. If you are walking from Kether to Chokmah and you have drawn Judgement, then the exercise is now to experience Judgement as it relates to moving from the Crown to Wisdom.

4. Do steps 5 through 7 from Pathworking Exercise 1 for the card and the path you have selected.

Herbalism Exercise

This exercise is for an herbalist or anyone who does esoteric work with plants and herbs and who wishes to combine herbal studies and tarot studies. Use a tarot or other deck that corresponds to herbs or plants, such as the Herbal Tarot, the Flower Speaks deck, or the Druid Plant Oracle. This exercise allows the cards to influence you as an herbalist, letting these two parts of your life interconnect.

To begin, you should be in your kitchen or wherever you make herbal recipes.

1. Center yourself using deep, cleansing breaths.

2. Shuffle the cards and lay them out as shown in illustration 8.

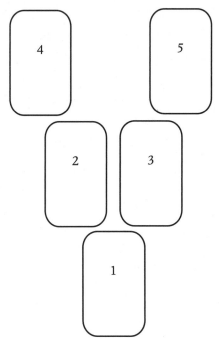

Illustration 8: Herbal Layout

3. These five cards will be five ingredients of an incense, tea, or sa-
    chet. Each card will represent a single ingredient. For example,
    if you're using the Herbal Tarot and draw the High Priest, the
    ingredient is sage. Once you've laid out the cards, assemble the
    five ingredients that the five cards represent.

4. Meditate with your ingredients: What is their purpose? How best
    can they be used? What instruction is the card layout actually giv-
    ing to you?

5. Use your final product: burn the incense, drink the tea, or do
    whatever you were guided to do.

Omen Exercise

Depending on your spiritual bent, it may be that you are someone who pays attention to signs in nature and the world around you. For example, you may have spirit guides or angels who send messages through such omens. If so, you can use the tarot to enhance this experience and to seek guidance on a specific matter. Even if this isn't normally a part of your life, you can use this exercise to open yourself to natural signs.

You can use any tarot deck for this exercise, but it will be enhanced if you select a deck that connects to your spiritual tradition, as described in the "Cultural Disciplines" section earlier in this chapter.

Obviously, you can receive an omen and draw a card (or several cards) to interpret it. But this exercise is a little different.

1. Center yourself using deep, cleansing breaths.

2. Say a prayer or make whatever spirit contact is usual for you, requesting guidance.

3. Clearly state your question out loud. You should know exactly what you're asking for. For example, "I have received a job offer. Please send me a sign if I should accept it."

4. Take another moment to breathe calmly and slowly and open yourself to your spirit guides.

5. Shuffle your cards.

6. Draw a single card and gaze at it. One image will pop out for you. For example, suppose you use the Classic Tarot and draw Temperance (illustration 9). You may see the irises by the waterside.

Illustration 9: Temperance
(Classic Tarot)

7. Your sign, then, is an iris, or perhaps a yellow flower, depending on how you perceive it. As you go about the next day or so, seeing your sign (whatever it is) will be the affirmative answer you requested. Otherwise, the answer is no.

Dream-Induction Exercise

A lot of people who work with esoteric disciplines work with dream states, including lucid dreaming, dream interpretation, and dream induction. This exercise is meant for someone who is already interested in dreams. Perhaps you keep a dream diary, perhaps you have had a dream or dreams that proved prophetic, or perhaps you have an interest in altered states of consciousness in general.

This exercise requires a journal or notebook, which will be used for recording your results.

Note that any dream exercise—this one or any other—works best if you do not wake up to an alarm clock. Waking naturally is the best way to remember your dreams and be able to record them.

Do this exercise immediately before going to sleep, right before you turn off the light. Do not read, play with your phone, or do anything else once you have completed the exercise.

1. As usual, begin by taking some cleansing breaths and centering yourself.

2. Shuffle your cards.

3. Say out loud, "This card will be in my dreams tonight." Turn over one card.

4. Study the card closely. Note images on the card, as well as the feelings the card invokes in you.

5. Write down the date and the name of the card (and the deck, if you use more than one) in your journal, as well as your impressions.

6. Say, "[Name of card] will be in my dreams tonight."

7. Turn off the light and go to sleep.

8. In the morning, record whatever you remember of your dreams in your journal. Do this before getting out of bed.

9. Repeat this exercise on a regular basis and record the results.

Writing Exercise

In the "Other Disciplines" section earlier in this chapter, we touched upon the wide array of life interests, hobbies, and studies that could influence your choice of a tarot deck and shape your interaction with the tarot. One such interest is writing—one particularly close to my own heart. This exercise is for writers.

Choose any tarot deck, or select one with a literary theme, such as those listed in the "Other Disciplines" section.

1. Select a piece of your writing that could use some direction— something you're blocked on, or something that feels stagnant or

uninspired. It can be fiction or nonfiction. You can be completely stuck, or just moving slowly or without a spark.

2. Place a paper copy of this piece of writing before you, open to the last page. If you have been unable to begin writing, a blank page representing the unstarted project can be used.

3. Center yourself with several deep, slow, cleansing breaths.

4. Shuffle the cards while thinking about the writing project. Don't try to create or determine what you'll write next; just allow the subject matter to fill your mind.

5. Place three cards in a row, from left to right, on top of your manuscript (or blank page), as shown in illustration 10.

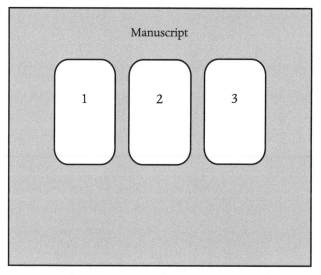

Illustration 10: Three Cards on the Manuscript

6. Use these cards as your inspiration. You can consider them the beginning, middle, and end, or just three inspiring cards. Begin writing about what you see on the first card, what it means to you in relation to this manuscript, and what it inspires within you. Don't worry about how it will fit into your overall writing project; just write about the inspiration.

7. Continue with the second and third cards.

8. If you feel like diving directly into your writing project as soon as you finish, go ahead. However, you can also sleep on it. Let the cards, their inspiration, and the write-up you just did satisfy you, and let your subconscious continue to work on it. After a night's sleep, reread what you wrote the day before during the exercise. You might find that it was exactly the awakening you needed.

THREE

Interaction
with Pattern

One of the simplest ways to expand your understanding of the meaning of a tarot layout is to look for frequency patterns in the cards. This is an additional component to a reading, separate from any individual card.

In other words, suppose you lay out a six-card reading, and four of those cards are cups.[3] This would give you, as a beginning, seven different things to say: the meanings of the six cards, and the meaning of two-thirds of those cards being cups. (You'll have far more than seven things to say by the end of this book!)

Do the Math

In order to recognize something as unusual, you have to know what your odds are, so we're going to have to crunch some numbers.

---

3. Note that the four suits of the tarot have a variety of names. I use wands, swords, cups, and pentacles. Wands can be batons or staves, swords can be spades, cups can be hearts, and pentacles can be disks or coins. Some unusual decks will assign different suits, such as the flamingos, peppermills, hats, and oysters of the Wonderland Tarot.

In a standard tarot deck, there are:

- 78 cards in total

- 22 major arcana cards ("trumps")—28 percent of a deck

- Suits: wands, pentacles, cups, and swords—each of which represents 18 percent of a deck. Each suit has:

    - 10 numbered cards

    - Court cards (usually pages, knights, queens, and kings)

- 20 percent of the deck is composed of court cards, so any one type of court card is 5 percent

- Each number from one through ten appears on 6 percent of the cards (once in each suit and once in the trumps)

Other recognizable patterns are harder to quantify because they vary from deck to deck, but we'll get to that.

This chart shows a normal distribution of cards in a reading:

Distribution of Cards			
	6-Card Reading	10-Card Reading	12-Card Reading
Majors	1–2	2–3	3–4
Each Suit	1–2	1–2	2–3
Court Card	1–2	2	2–3
Any Number 1–10	0–1	0–1	0–1

If you did a six-card reading, it would be normal to see two cups, but three would be slightly unusual, and four would be of real interest and worth adding a layer to your reading—worth interacting with.

Note that, for numbers, it is unusual to see more than one card of any number unless the reading has a *lot* of cards—more than twenty. We'll address number patterns a little later in this chapter.

Also note that the numbers in the table don't have to equal the total number of cards in a reading, since there will be overlap. For example, a

Knight of Swords would be counted as both a court card and a sword, while the Magician would count both as a major and as the number one.

Now, just as a card can have multiple meanings, so can a pattern. It is easy enough to say that cups represent love and emotion, but how that pattern interacts with the reading as a whole is up to you, the reader, to determine.

Suit Patterns

Here is a general overview of suit patterns:

- A pattern of swords indicates that the reading has a lot to do with aggression, conflict, speech, or argument, or that there is intense movement related to the reading.

- A pattern of wands indicates that the reading has a lot to do with building, creating, establishing, or labor.

- A pattern of cups indicates that the reading has a lot to do with love, emotions, or the subconscious.

- A pattern of pentacles indicates that the reading has a lot to do with money, career, or education.

But how do you apply these patterns to a reading? First, do the math; be comfortable knowing that you're really seeing a pattern. You'll second-guess yourself if you stop to ask yourself if this is truly an unusual distribution. That's the purpose of including the numeric data in this chapter. Once you've determined that there is indeed a pattern, there are several approaches you can take.

First, you can read a pattern as if it's another card.

Second, ask yourself how this pattern applies to this reading. Sometimes a suit confirms the subject of a reading (*Well, you're getting a lot of pentacles, which makes sense since you're asking about money*), but sometimes the pattern can provide redirection of the concern. Querents ask what they want to know, but if a deeper issue is behind the concern, that will come out in the reading. Querents may also be misunderstanding the situation (*Well, this card and this card confirm that it's a work situation, but the prevalence of cups elsewhere suggests that satisfaction and feeling play a larger role than money*).

Speaking of which, the third component is that *absence is as important as presence.*

Very often, a querent will ask for a "general life" reading, and I'll go through the process of telling him what's going on, and then he'll say, "Do you see a relationship?" That's the point at which you count up the cups. If there are a large number of cups, then you can say, even though the reading hadn't pointed to a relationship, that love may be coming. But most of the time, that's when I say, "There are no cups here," or "There's only one cup, and it's reversed."

If you read for the general public, or even just for your friends, you get used to the love question being the most common question you're asked. As a result, you learn to look for something that isn't there, to note absence, and to use absence as a significant point.

Also note that I incorporated the fourth component: How is the suit aspected? What is the context of the pattern? It's not just that my querent in the earlier paragraph had only one cup, it's that it was reversed. As you learn more about interactive reading, you'll learn more ways in which the suit can be affected by other cards. For now, note that if all the cards of a suit are negative or are placed negatively, then that's an important part of the pattern.

By "placed negatively," I mean that the card is next to, in conjunction with, or part of the meaning of a negative card or position. Chapter 4 will address position and layout in depth, and we'll get to cards functioning in conjunction with other cards in chapter 5.

A card is negative if the meaning itself is negative (as with the Three or Nine of Swords) or if it's reversed. There are some cards that are so positive that they shine through as positive even when reversed (such as the Four of Cups or the Ten of Pentacles), and there are cards for which the reversal is more positive than the upright (again, this is true of both the Three and Nine of Swords). However, when looking for patterns, it's important to stop and count reversals, just as you would count a suit or a number.

It's also important to note whether the pattern interacts with another pattern. Do you see both dominant suits and a pattern of reversals? Two dominant suits? A dominant suit and a lot of court cards? All of these are part of the context of the pattern.

Sample Reading: Dominant Suits

For sample readings in this book, I'm trying something a little daring: shuffling my deck and seeing what comes up. If my cards are true to me, they should bring readings that apply to the current lesson and enhance the meaning of each chapter. Unless otherwise noted, every reading in this book is either a real reading for a client or a sample reading I did on the fly, shuffling and laying out cards next to my desk.

Here's what I drew for a sample reading on interacting with a suit pattern (illustration 11):

Four of Pentacles — *Ace of Pentacles* — *Seven of Swords reversed* — *Three of Pentacles reversed* — *Ace of Swords*

Illustration 11: Sample Pattern Reading (Robin Wood Tarot)

Let's ignore the layout for now, since that's for a later chapter, and just look at the cards.

This is definitely an unusual reading, because we have only two suits and no majors. (Distribution is often unusual on a small reading because it's a small sample size. You can get an idea of the norms by looking at the distribution of cards chart from the last section and cutting the numbers for a ten-card reading in half.)

To summarize, here are the four components of reading a pattern:

1. Read a pattern as if it's another card.
2. Ask yourself how this pattern applies to this reading.
3. Absence is as important as presence.
4. What is the context of the pattern?

Read the Pattern as if It's Another Card

In my sample reading, I have pentacles and swords, with more pentacles. Swords can indicate conflict or movement, while pentacles can indicate money or career. Together, they tell me this reading is about competition or conflict on the job.

Note that I'm already interacting; I'm looking at the combination of swords and pentacles and asking where they intersect. That meeting place tells me a story about this reading.

Reading the pattern as if it's another card means that "conflict on the job" is treated as a card meaning, just like "greed or short-sighted-ness" (the meaning of the Four of Pentacles).

Ask Yourself How This Pattern Applies to This Reading

We don't have a question on the table, but that's not uncommon. If you read for yourself, you always know the question. But whenever a querent is involved, she might choose to withhold the question, either because she's embarrassed or because she doesn't wish to taint the reading with foreknowledge. In fact, many readers *request* that the querent withhold the question for that reason. If prior information serves as a barrier to the free flow of your intuition, where your psyche says "X" but your conscious mind says "X can't be right because I have been told YZ," then you can choose to read without any question asked in advance. Then at some point during the reading, once information is flowing and you've gotten some positive feedback ("Yep, this is what I was silently asking about"), you can ask the querent what it was all about.

Nonetheless, I know what the reading is about by understanding the pattern in the first place. It's about career conflict—which I learned by reading the suit pattern as a card. Now I can go back and read the cards, and ask how this pattern affects the implied question.

One thing we see is that pentacles slightly dominate swords—there are more of them, suggesting that the career itself is the most important part of the reading, not the conflict that is currently occurring. I should keep this in mind as I read each individual card.

Absence Is as Important as Presence

What is missing from this reading? In a five-card reading, it is natural that all sorts of things won't appear—there just isn't room. Note absence as it comes up in relation to the reading, or to questions that the querent may have.

Is the reading about love? Nope. If the querent wants to know if people's feelings are hurt at work, or if it's an issue of morale, the answer is no. Any of these things would be indicated by cups, and there are none.

If the querent is trying to pinpoint an individual—the boss or a coworker—you can point out that there are no court cards. The only dominant person in this reading is the fellow depicted in the Seven of Swords. I say this because the person depicted in the Seven of Swords has committed a deceitful or dishonorable act, perhaps a theft. This person's identity and/or behavior will be important in the reading. Two other cards have pictures of people, but in both cases, the people seem to be indicating abstract concepts, not individuals. While the Three and Four of Pentacles show people, their meanings reside in situations.

They might refer to people, but they don't have to. I'm not seeing cards that indicate gossip (like the Three of Cups) or power (like the Emperor), so I don't think the situation is interpersonal or about authority.

Speaking of absence, there are also no majors, suggesting a certain impermanence or pettiness in the situation.

THE CONTEXT OF THE PATTERN

The first and most obvious context is that there is a second pattern: there are two aces. In such a small reading, any repeated number is very significant.

Aces have to do with beginnings; getting things started. In relation to the suit pattern (work and conflict), it seems like the primary issue has to do with starting something new: a work conflict in regard to a beginning—perhaps a new project, a new source of income, a new investment, or a new competitor.

There's no particular pattern of reversals. Three reversals and two upright cards suggest a slightly more negative than positive energy, but it's not a dominant pattern: 1/4 or 0/5 in either direction would be more notable.

But look at how the reversals interact with the other patterns: pentacles have the negative ace, and swords have the positive ace. Could it be that confronting the conflict directly and forcefully, rather than pushing the financial interests, is a solution?

Now take a moment to see that we've already gathered a huge amount of information, and we *haven't read a single card*. We haven't engaged with the meaning of any particular card in detail. Simply by looking at patterns—at suits, numbers, absence, presence, and reversals— we've learned a great deal about this reading.

We know it's about a work conflict, and that the conflict involves starting something new. We know the situation isn't about emotions or anything interpersonal. We know the energy around the situation has been negative, but we can see a possible solution. We know that confronting the problem verbally and assertively is likely to work better than focusing on the financial aspects of the new beginning (whatever it is).

This is an impressive start to a reading, and we have yet to look at the card meanings. There's a thief in the center, a situation involving short-sightedness and greed, and perhaps issues of recognition and reward. All of this is seen when we start looking at specific cards, but our understanding of each—the Four of Pentacles is the miser, the Seven of Swords is the thief, and the Three of Pentacles is the craftsman who may not be getting recognition—is colored by reading the pattern.

Reversals

There are readers who never use reversals in their readings. In general, they give two reasons: one, that it overcomplicates the reading, doubling the number of possible meanings, and two, that it is too negative. I don't like either of these reasons. The first I reject because I think life is incredibly complicated and full of shades of gray, and that the best way to offer a truly useful reading is to apply your psychic skills in an environment where you can choose among a full array of life situations. A full astrological chart reading is more accurate than a simple sun sign interpretation because your moment and location of birth are uniquely your own, whereas a sun sign reading applies to about one-twelfth of all people. The more complex potential a reading has, the truer it is to the individual. As to the second reason, I also think that life brings us negativity, challenges, and disruptions—if it didn't, tarot readers would have far fewer querents! Negative meanings help to accurately reflect life as we all experience it.

Some readers say that they just know (intuitively or psychically) whether to draw on the negative or positive meaning of a card, and don't need reversals. Fair enough, but the whole purpose of the cards, in my view, is to utilize a complex interface between your inner psychic abilities and the rest of the world. In other words, if you just know, that's fine, but I think that the more the cards show you, the more your psychic abilities are empowered to know more and different things.

In order to make sure that a reading has a good, randomized assortment of upright and reversed cards, I flip the deck with each shuffle. I split the deck in two, flip one half end to end, shuffle, and repeat each time. I do this so routinely that I've been caught doing the flip when playing card games with my family!

Reversals impact both individual cards and the overall patterns in a reading, and should be looked at with that in mind. Just as any given card is itself *and* its suit (which can form a pattern) *and* its number (which can form a pattern), it is also both itself and its upright or reversed nature.

My understanding of reversals is, perhaps, unique. I see upright cards as inherently stable and reversals as inherently unstable. Visualize each card as a structure; if the card is reversed, that structure is standing on its head!

Illustration 12: Two of Cups, Upright and Reversed (Universal Tarot)

Look at the Two of Cups (illustration 12). Upright, these two people are standing on their feet and are likely to stay on their feet. Reversed, they're balanced on their heads! This is unstable and the whole situation is likely to topple.

Just as those two people are more comfortable on their feet than on their heads, and want to be on their feet, I find that any reversal wants to be upright. This is important because when querents see negative information in a reading, they naturally want to know what the solution is. The solution to a reversal is usually to set the card upright, and you can even show the querent how much more natural the situation would be when set aright by briefly taking the card out of the layout and turning it upright.

In other words, don't grasp outside of that card for a solution; the solution is in the card itself—it's in flipping that card back over!

You can think of a reversal, then, as a card interacting with itself.

But on to pattern. If you've randomized reversals as I suggest (or by some other means), it would be normal to see approximately half of the reading reversed, and random distribution would allow for that to vary, plus or minus, to some degree. You're looking for extreme cases—when two-thirds or more of the reading is upright or reversed.

In the next chapter, we'll look at a reading that calls for an exact count of reversals, but for pattern recognition, a number range is all you need. A ten-card reading with seven or eight reversals shows a significant and unusual pattern. Whatever else you know about the reading and the cards, you know it is trending toward reversal.

What does that mean? The meaning of the reading can be negative or dark, or unstable in the way that individual reversals are unstable. Specific cards or other patterns will guide you.

A reading might have reversals plus a preponderance of a suit, or a dominant suit might also be reversed. These are two different things.

For example, the following two readings[4] (illustrations 13 and 14) show different patterns.

The pattern in the first reading (illustration 13) indicates a dominance of wands, and also a strong negative trend. Each suit has a reversed card. The reversal trend isn't about any one suit, and, in fact, is global.

---

4. In order to show how the pattern changes, I constructed these sample readings, unlike other readings in the book, which are all real readings drawn randomly.

Nine of Wands   *Six of Swords reversed*   *Ten of Wands reversed*

Four of Cups reversed   *Two of Wands*   *Five of Pentacles reversed*

Illustration 13: Reversals Plus a Dominant Suit (Classic Tarot)

The pattern in the second reading (illustration 14) places the negativity squarely in the domain of wands—wands are the cause or location of the negativity.

Remember the four parts of reading a pattern. As with suits, reversals are meaningful in their absence as well as their presence. A reading without any reversals predicts an unusually positive outcome, even if the cards also indicate problems or struggles.

Nine of Wands reversed   Six of Swords   Ten of Wands reversed

Four of Cups   Two of Wands reversed   Five of Pentacles reversed

Illustration 14: Reversals in a Dominant Suit (Classic Tarot)

Major Arcana

Many readers treat the majors as a very different animal from the minors. There are even decks consisting entirely of the twenty-two major arcana, omitting the minors.

In general, the majors are considered to be more important. Depending on who you ask, this is because they represent the soul's journey through life, or the querent's fate, or the will of God. Most tarot teachers will point out that the majors, read in order, tell a tale of the journey of a person from individual ego to ascended spirit, from the Magician to the

World, through which the soul wanders hither and yon like an unnumbered Fool. For the Jungian, the majors are a psychological journey of self-actualization, and for the Kabbalist, each major is a path on the Tree of Life.

My primary concern has always been as a reader and not as a mystic. I see the majors as I see the minors: components of a reading.

A preponderance of major arcana indicates that large forces are at play. The querent may have little control over the events that are unfolding. A lot of majors in a reading may indicate the following:

- The subjects depicted in the reading are life-changing events that will affect the querent for years to come.
- The querent may have little control over the outcome; the matter may be in the hands of fate.
- The querent is at a crossroads; decisions made now will determine the querent's future.
- The majors may indicate life lessons that must be learned.

By contrast, an absence of majors can indicate that the events are just ordinary life events, and no big deal in the grand scheme of things.

When a reading is difficult, challenging, or really dark, the querent will want to know how to get out of it and what to change. A pattern of majors indicates that applying willpower is not going to help. Depending on the specific cards, this may be a time to accept the experience as a lesson, or as fate, or it may be a time for prayer or meditation.

By the way, expect plenty of majors when reading for adolescents; their lives are in constant dramatic flux, and almost every day is a turning point.

Number Patterns

Numbers are a complicated subject to address because there are so many systems of numerology. Still, it's important, because any number pattern is significant. With each number from one to ten appearing on only 6 percent of the cards, two or three instances of the same number in a reading is definitely a pattern worth noting.

By "number pattern," I mean a pattern of the same number appearing over and over. Even twice is notable unless you're doing a very large reading—twenty-four cards or more. I've never worked with actual *patterns*, as in a sequence of numbers, or noticing a reading of only even or odd numbers, or whatever. Theoretically, it's certainly possible to find meaning in that, and if such a pattern speaks to you, go for it!

Keep in mind the principles of reading patterns. We've looked previously at an example of an ace pattern interacting with a reading. If you are already conversant in a numerology system, use the one you know. Otherwise, take my brief descriptions as a guide.

Aces—Keyword "Beginning"

Aces are beginnings, as discussed in the sample reading in illustration 11. They represent something new that has come or will come into the querent's life, or the effort to create something new, or, in the case of reversals, the difficulties or challenges encountered when attempting to create something new. The Magician, which is the number one in the major arcana, is creative power and therefore the potential to begin anything.

Twos—Keywords "Duality" and "Balance"

Twos can represent balance, duality, or stasis. Each two in the tarot has the quality of *On the one hand …, but on the other hand …* The manifestation of that paired-ness can be stasis (Two of Swords), waiting (Two of Wands), a meeting of minds (Two of Cups), juggling (Two of Pentacles), or the Pillars of Justice and Mercy (High Priestess). In each case, a quality of paired or dual energy is encountered and must be faced—with love, anticipation, or panic, but it must be faced.

Threes—Keywords "Outcome" and "Flux"

Three is an outcome. An egg (one) plus a seed (two) equals a child (three); the fertile outcome that may or may not occur is the overarching meaning of three in a reading. Threes can also indicate a state of flux; pyramids have a solid base and an unstable tip, and love triangles are prone to breaking apart. Three creates and can destroy.

Fours—Keyword "Possession"

Fours are stable just as threes are unstable; they represent reality, possessions, and results. If three is the child of the family, then four is the house in which the family lives. Fours in the minor arcana address different responses to the material world: the sword withdraws, the wand celebrates, the cup questions, and the pentacle grasps. In the major arcana, the Emperor is mastery over the material.

Fives—Keyword "Change"

In the tarot, the fives of the minor arcana all depict changes in circumstances; there is a great deal of uncertainty and upheaval, while the five in the major arcana, the Hierophant, is almost reactionary in its distrust of any sort of change. The Hierophant is the ultimate conservative of the tarot. Fives move and are active, but they can also be unhappy. Of course, any card in the tarot can be unhappy based on placement and other aspects, but five is a roiling energy that can have unhappiness as its natural companion.

Sixes—Keyword "Journey"

In the tarot, six starts to observe life conditions and stabilize them. Any double in numerology tends to exalt or stabilize its earlier form, so six is a more solid three. In the minors, journeying is a theme of the six: both swords and wands depict a physical journey, cups depict a journey into memory or into the past, and pentacles show a more metaphorical journey—of social position. In the majors, six is the Lovers, which can be a journey toward love, but doesn't necessarily represent a journey. Even though the Lovers card diverges from the lesson of the minors, if it appears in a reading with another six, it should be noted.

Sevens—Keyword "Willpower"

Seven is a number of great mystical significance. In the tarot, the sevens tend to describe willpower and self-control, and their manifestation in various aspects of life. You can read this at a higher level, as the soul exalting itself through will, or you can just use the keyword as a guide to a pattern of sevens appearing in a reading. The Seven of Swords is a dissolute and dishonest will, and the wands show combat and high ground—the will to succeed, fight back, and win. The Seven of Cups is a dissipated and confused will; the inability to apply will is suggested. The pentacles manifest as hard work, the will to create work, and satisfaction (or its lack) with the result. The Chariot, number seven in the majors, is the application of willpower in life generally, and the need to control out-of-control situations.

Eights—Keyword "Progress"

In the tarot, eights depict progress and strength, which is apropos considering that Strength is the eighth major in any Waite-based deck. (It is eleventh in Thoth-based decks, but for that system, you'll need a different book.) The Eight of Swords is the trap, the inability to progress, and the absence of strength. The Eight of Wands is the opposite, depicting rapid, headlong movement forward. The Eight of Cups is a kind of progress *away*—from materialism or from sorrow. The Eight of Pentacles is educational or career progress, and depicts a student excelling in his studies. All of these are examples of life progressing and strength being needed. (Absence, we know, is as significant as presence, and here the cards show us the same thing, as swords represent the absence of the qualities of eights.)

Nines—Keyword "Fulfillment"

Nine is three times three, so we can take three's keyword, "outcome," and call nine "outcome of outcome." It pushes these cards almost to their ultimate manifestation (which will be complete at ten). In the tarot, nines are showing us the material result of the suit, so that the Nine of Swords is the outcome of swords (despair), and so on with all four suits. The ninth major is the Hermit, which is almost an outcome of its own—if the first seven majors depict physical fulfillment and Strength begins an inner journey, then the Hermit is the outcome—seeking wisdom.

Tens—Keyword "Completion"

Each of the suits is now done. We've come to the end of our pack of ten. Each ten takes the final step to complete the journey that seemed finished at nine. If the Nine of Swords is despair, then the Ten of Swords is total defeat. Both the Ten of Cups and Ten of Pentacles are happier and lovelier than the Nines, while the Ten of Swords and Ten of Wands are darker.

The ten in the major arcana is the Wheel of Fortune, indicating that when we come to completion, we go back around again.

Remember that a number pattern can be read as an additional card, it can interact with what is already known about the reading, and it should be viewed in the context of how and where it appears and if there are reversals connected to the pattern. The principle "Absence is as important as presence" is less meaningful with numbers, because any repeated number is rare. Nonetheless, look for absences that you think are significant.

Sometimes you have a psychic question instead of a psychic answer. You get a sort of *I wonder if this means…* in your head. That's when you look for other cards that would confirm your idea, and their absence can redirect your psychic energy.

For example, if you see a pattern of sevens, you know the issue has something to do with the querent's will or focus. Is it about romance? A moral choice? Work? The presence or absence of other cards will help guide you. A moral choice will almost certainly be accompanied by major arcana; if there's no Lovers, Devil, or Temperance, you can probably eliminate that option. So, when looking at number patterns, you're not just looking for absence or presence of numbers, but for absence or presence of other, supporting cards.

Presence of People

Court cards are a sticking point for a lot of people, a place where even experienced readers can get blocked or confused.[5] This isn't a lesson in how to read court cards, though, but in how to read a profusion of court cards and people in a reading.

People in a reading? Most tarot cards depict people. I went through a Waite deck and counted only the cards that showed people with clearly visible faces. While there's room for disagreement about my definition, omitting the court cards, I counted twenty-five minors out of forty and seventeen majors out of twenty-two. Since most of the tarot, in most decks, consists of images of people, it would be weird to single that out as a pattern.

Sometimes, though, when you have a lot of court cards in a reading, you'll also start to notice that other cards *seem* more like people and less like symbols. This is your psychic wisdom noticing the pattern and seeing it reinforced.

People in a reading mean just that: people. One of the things that is confusing about reading a single court card is determining if it means a person, or if it represents the querent, or if it's a condition, a state of mind, a situation, or what. But when a high percentage of the reading is populated by court cards, there can be no doubt that a lot of people are around the situation.

This can mean all sorts of things, of course, and, as with any other pattern, you're going to look for placement and other cards to help you determine exactly what's going on. Suit makes a difference, obviously, as does the particular member of the court. But whatever the specific meaning, start with the understanding that these are people.

In a reading, it's easy to get bogged down trying to figure out who such-and-such court card represents. *Is that my father? My boss? My ex-boyfriend?* Sometimes you know right away, and sometimes a few pointed questions will get you there, but often, you can just let it go. Describe the

---

5. The court cards are the page, knight, queen, and king in Waite-based decks, or the princess, knight, queen, and prince in Thoth-based decks. There are many variations on these titles in other decks.

circumstances, energy, and ideas that come from this card, and ultimately the identity will reveal itself—maybe even after the reading.

What a reading crowded with court cards says is that *people are important here*. This isn't a situation happening in the querent's head; it's not a delusion. Or it could be pointing to support. This person is definitely not alone, so the court may be playing a supportive role: loaning money, lending a friendly ear, or providing opportunities, education, pressure, or guilt. The support can be positive or negative, but it's definitely there.

Sample Reading: Court Cards

Here's a sample reading involving the court cards (illustration 15). In a seven-card reading, a court card should show up once or twice (1.4 times on average), so you wouldn't note this as remarkable—except for the fact that both court cards in this reading are knights, which is not at all likely, so this should be treated as a pattern.

There's a lot going on in this reading, with both majors reversed, a card of conflict (Five of Wands reversed) and a card of great sorrow (Nine of Swords). With all this gloom and drama, we need to note the pattern—that men in the querent's life play a notable role in the goings-on. These men appear to be opposed to each other (one reversed, one upright) or coming from opposite sides of the table. The querent is somehow between them. (If you use a significator—a card pulled from the deck and placed on the table to represent the querent—it is always placed in the center. Even if you don't use a significator, the center of the reading is where you should consider your querent to be located.)

As with the previous sample reading, we're looking only at the patterns, not doing the reading yet (and this is a sample reading, not a live client reading). Reversals, majors, and suits are all normally distributed, and no number is repeated. The only unusual pattern, then, is the knights, but you already know something important.

The sense that "there are a lot of people" might lead you to look differently at the other cards. The Five of Wands in reverse starts to look less like a metaphor for conflict and more like actual men in combat, since two men are seen elsewhere in the reading.

Illustration 15: Knights in a Reading (Robin Wood Tarot)

Other Patterns

Other symbols that are present in a card reading will vary widely depending on the specific deck and your perception as a reader. You can expect to see paths, mountains, rocks, waves, fields, various animals, wind, clouds, specific colors, fruit, or the absence of any of these. In a reading, this may be something you notice in a specific card, as with the Queen of Pentacles in chapter 1 (illustration 2). But right now we're looking for patterns. If a path appears repeatedly, you can be sure that there is a way out of current difficulties, and if there's no path on any card, that tells you something as well.

None of these symbols are complicated or obscure. Ordinary spoken language will tell you the meaning of most "background" symbols. "The sun is shining on me" is symbolic of happiness, good fortune, and clarity, while "clouds over my head" indicates a dark mood and bad luck. You knew the meaning of such phrases long before you picked up a deck of cards!

Let's go back to the sample reading at the beginning of this chapter (illustration 11). You'll recall that this reading had three pentacles and two swords. The Robin Wood deck, following Waite's example, associates swords with air (some decks associate swords with fire, but sword/air is more common). Naturally, with swords, you're going to expect air imagery, but three of the five cards in this reading show clouds—both swords and the Four of Pentacles. In addition, the craftsman in the Three of Pentacles is Daedalus, working on a pair of giant wings! The air imagery is clearly a pattern. Air is associated with language and ideas, and clouds are associated with troubles. These images reinforce our earlier conclusion that the reading suggests a solution based in swords and in direct confrontation. The clouds repeat our understanding that there are troubles and conflicts, while the overall preponderance of air echoes our previous conclusion that direct confrontation is needed by indicating that the confrontation should be verbal.

Let's look at the reading in illustration 15. Are there any repeated symbols in these cards? I notice that two cards show people standing on the brown earth: the Knight of Pentacles and Death. (While it's actually the Knight's horse that is standing on the earth, a knight and his horse are almost one being in the tarot.) The Knight's earth is a cultivated field, and Death's is a path. While fields and paths have different symbolic meanings, it's intriguing to see this intersection between these two cards.

The Robin Wood Tarot: The Book has a section on the symbols to be found in this deck. It includes various colors, items like books or chains, a variety of plants, and things like paths, clouds, and fields. What it *doesn't* include is an entry for "earth," "dirt," or "soil."

If you noticed the soil as a repeated element and then looked it up in the book, it would be easy to become uncertain and say to yourself, "I must have been wrong." By now you should know, though, that this type of thinking silences the Psychic Child. If the idea of "earth" as a symbol is something that seems right to you as you read it in the layout, then there's something there to be discovered. This is one reason to read off-book as soon as you can (while still maintaining your studies).

Homework

In the introduction, I stated that you should memorize the basic meanings of each card, using card-by-card interpretation books, the short meanings in appendix A, and/or the little booklet that comes with any deck. By this point, that task should already be complete. If it isn't, you may wish to pause in your reading and get to work!

Journal

Begin keeping a journal of tarot readings. This can be handwritten, or you can take pictures of your readings and jot down notes electronically, or whatever other method works for you. The purpose is to mark your progress as you move through the exercises in this book, and to give you a sense of your accuracy and connection to the cards over time.

Distribution

Your homework now is to memorize the Distribution of Cards chart at the beginning of this chapter. When you see a layout, you should immediately understand if a pattern appears.

Patterns

You should also work to memorize the keywords for numbers, suits, and the presence of court and major arcana cards that appear in this chapter.

Homework Questions

You should be able to answer the following questions without referring to the Distribution of Cards chart at the beginning of this chapter.

1. You have laid out ten cards:

   • There are four swords, two pentacles, two cups, one wand, and one major.

   • Four cards are reversed and six are upright.

   • There are no court cards.

   • No two cards with the same number appear.

What is unusual about this reading?

2. In addition to the meanings ascribed to the following cards, what keywords might apply to them?

   a. The High Priestess

   b. The King of Pentacles

   c. The Six of Swords

   d. The Ace of Cups

Oracle Card Homework

If you use an oracle (non-tarot) deck, the distribution offered in the previous homework section will not apply to you, nor will the homework questions. In that case, your task is to figure out for yourself what number patterns are meaningful in your own deck. For example, if you use the Cards of Alchemy deck, there are five suits with nine cards in each, plus five "wild cards." So each suit is 18 percent of the deck, and wild cards are 10 percent. In a ten-card reading, one wild card is the normal distribution, and zero and two are both in range.

Your homework: Determine the distribution pattern in your own oracle deck, if any, and memorize it.

Homework Answers

1. In this distribution, the (four) swords are a pattern. The absence of court cards is unusual. Only one major is probably a pattern (but not an extreme one) and should be kept in mind. Reversals are normal. Number cards are normal.

2. Keywords for these cards could be:

    a. The High Priestess: balance/duality (a two) and fate (a major).

    b. The King of Pentacles: people or men (a court card) and career or money (a pentacle).

    c. The Six of Swords: aggression (a sword) and journey (a six).

    d. The Ace of Cups: beginnings (an ace) and love (a cup).

Exercise

This exercise will guide you through a reading such as the Dominant Suits sample reading earlier in this chapter (see illustration 11). You will be doing a reading based solely on pattern, without reading the meanings of the cards or their positions. You may, if you wish, read the card meanings after the exercise is done, but it will be important, at first, to completely disregard those meanings so that you focus your full psychic and cognitive attention on patterns.

1. Begin with several deep, cleansing breaths, and center yourself.

2. Ask your question out loud. For this exercise, keep it simple. For example, it can be "How will my day go tomorrow?"

3. Shuffle the cards until you feel it's time to stop.

4. Lay out five cards as follows, in the order indicated (illustration 16):

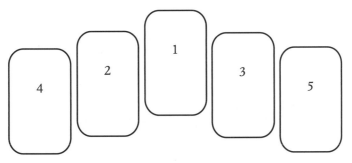

Illustration 16: Pattern Exercise

5. Start by counting reversals. The general tenor of the reading can be gauged instantly in a reading with an odd number of cards.

More than half are either upright or reversed, so you can start by determining if the overall tone is positive or negative, stable or unstable.

6. Now it's time to look at suits. If you've done your homework, you'll know that in a five-card reading you should notice any suit that appears more than once, and the majors if they appear more than twice.

7. Now notice any numbers that appear more than once.

8. Notice if there is more than one court card.

9. Now take note of anything that is completely absent. It's normal for a suit to be absent in a five-card reading, and it's normal for any number to be absent.

10. For each pattern you have found, read it as if it's another card. It will help to describe the meaning of the pattern out loud. You may also wish to write it down in your journal, or you may wish to save the journaling until you are finished.

11. Ask yourself how this pattern applies to this reading. How does this pattern interact with, for example, how your day will go tomorrow?

12. Absence is as important as presence: Ask yourself what is missing and how that will impact the subject of the reading.

13. What is the context of the pattern? Is the pattern associated with reversed or upright cards? Are there multiple patterns interacting with one another?

14. See if you can draw a conclusion about the reading. What is the outcome?

15. Only now should you consider the actual meanings of the cards.

16. If you haven't already done so, record the reading in your journal.

17. Repeat this exercise several times until you feel confident in your ability to read patterns.

FOUR

Interactions
with Layout and Position

Most of the time, when you read cards, you're reading them in a set layout. Therefore, the card's meaning must interact with the position of the card within that layout. This is the beginning of truly interactive tarot, as cards change meaning and tone from here on out. As we move in our study of cards through interactions with their positions, and, in our next chapters, with each other and with the story being told, we'll see that an infinite number of meanings can be discovered, not through memorization (which would be impossible) but through a moment-by-moment unfolding.

Types of Layouts

There are probably as many, if not more, card layouts (also called "spreads") as there are available decks. Readers make up their own all the time, and you can even make them up on the fly. Layouts can be complex, encompassing a whole life, in the way that an astrological chart can be used to read a person's life (there are tarot readings based on astrological charts, too). Other spreads can be deceptively simple.

Personally, I favor shorter, more direct layouts. Over the years, I've come to structure consultations around multiple short layouts rather than one big "tell me everything" layout, but this is entirely a personal preference.

A spread can cover every possible situation, or it can be simple and broad. You can have a general position like "nearby influence" or a detailed series of cards in positions for "unknown influence," "unknown danger," "influence of fate," and so on. It's good to have at least a few layouts in your repertoire that cover different needs in a reading. I have four or five such spreads I go to again and again, despite having studied many more than those.

Think of layouts in terms of the need they fulfill.

1. A full-life chart layout.
2. A snapshot layout: What's going on right now?
3. A decision layout: What should I/the querent do?

Full-Life Layouts

As I said, this spread is like reading a birth chart, and one method of doing this reading is to lay out the cards exactly as if it were an astrological chart. Obviously, if you're an astrologer, this is going to be a great reading to add to your bag of tricks.

The method is simple enough: Shuffle the deck and lay out one card for each astrological house, beginning in the first house (in the nine o'clock position) and going around all twelve houses counterclockwise. Then read each card as if it's in the house. You can even overlay known information about the querent's chart onto the reading. For example, my Sun is in my seventh house, so you could add an extra "Sun" card to the seventh position. (I don't mean to pull out the major arcana Sun, I mean a randomly drawn card representing the astrological "planet" of Sun.)

Some people use only major arcana for full-life readings, and some use a deck that includes only twenty-two cards for such readings.

Another full-life method is to shuffle the twenty-two majors and lay out all of them, reading in order as if the cards tell the story of a journey from birth to today, or from birth to a date in the future that you pick.

Full-life readings aren't something I use in my own tarot practice, so I don't have a lot of insight to share. If this type of reading interests you, you'll find there are many excellent resources. Eden Gray's *Mastering the Tarot*, for example, has a section on a horoscope-type reading. You'll find that the information explored in this chapter about other layouts will illuminate your work with full-life readings, if you choose to explore them.

Snapshot Layouts

These kinds of spreads give a picture of the querent's life as it is right now. Generally, they include information about the past and future, not just the present. Sometimes a snapshot will include information about what the querent might or should do, giving it some overlap with a decision layout. Most beginning readers start with a variation on the Celtic Cross layout, which is a snapshot spread.

Past-Present-Future Layout

Note: I would not advise using a significator in a three-card reading.

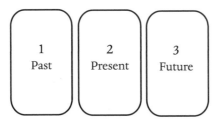

Illustration 17: Three-Card Snapshot: Past-Present-Future Layout

A three-card Past-Present-Future reading is about as simple a snapshot as can be. I often use it in conjunction with other layouts (more on that in a bit).

Shuffle or mix the cards, and lay one card in each position in the order shown (illustration 17). The card on the left represents the past, the center card is the present, and the right-hand card is the future.

How a Card Changes in a Position

The Past-Present-Future reading gives us the easiest way to understand how the meaning of a card changes in a position: the tense changes. Here are a couple of examples: [6]

Ten of Swords: *Defeat.*

Ten of Swords in the Past: *In the past, you were defeated.*

Ten of Swords in the Present: *You are currently experiencing a defeat; you feel utterly defeated right now; a recent defeat is affecting you currently.*

Ten of Swords in the Future: *You are about to face a major defeat; a situation you are entering into will end in your defeat; the competition or combat you are currently experiencing will end in your defeat.*

Hanged Man Reversed: *Unwillingness to face the hard work needed in order to achieve a goal; laziness; taking the easy way out.*

Hanged Man Reversed in the Past: *In the past, you chose an easier path; you skipped out on some hard work.*

Hanged Man Reversed in the Present: *You are not willing to face the hard work needed in order to achieve your goals; you are avoiding personal sacrifice.*

Hanged Man Reversed in the Future: *You are going to face the need to work very hard, at personal sacrifice, in order to achieve a goal, and it looks like you will be unwilling to do that.*

These are very simple interpretations of how reading a card changes based on position. It's easy to realize that placing "defeat" in the past

---

6. For the rest of the book, the sample readings will, of necessity, give card meanings. They may not be the meanings you've learned. The important thing to focus on is how the meaning of a card changes during tarot interactions. If you wish to apply this understanding to a different interpretation of a card, that's great.

means "you were defeated." This simple example, though, will pave the way for more complex shifts based on position.

At this point, these cards are still kind of hanging in space, standing alone with their meaning. You have shifted the meaning of a card based on where the card is, but it is not yet truly interactive.

The most important thing to understand about a layout is that *all the cards are in the same layout*. They are connected. They interact.

Let's use the exact same layout, but change how we describe the cards (illustration 18).

Now you can see that the layout is not three unrelated cards, and the cards do not depict just any past, or any future. Everything comes down to the present moment. The present is a lens through which we view the past and see the future.

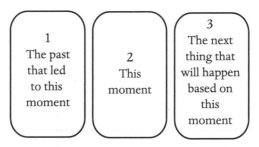

Illustration 18: Renaming Past-Present-Future

Usually, the interaction between past and present in a reading is "and therefore" or "but now." Any card in the present condition that can flow naturally from the card in the past condition is an "and therefore" interaction. Any card in the present that seems to contradict the past is a "but now."

Let's look at a couple of past-present combinations:

Past: Ten of Swords/Present: The Sun: *In the past, you were defeated, <u>but now</u> you feel a new day is dawning, and you're finally ready to let go of the wound you suffered.*

Past: Ten of Swords/Present: Nine of Wands: *In the past, you were defeated, <u>and therefore</u>, you are now guarded, cautious, and distrustful.*

You don't actually have to say the words "but now" or "and there-fore," but if it helps you focus on the interaction between past and present, then do so.

The interaction with the future is often also "and therefore." It can be "watch out for" as well. If a future outcome is negative, I like to show the querent her options. In the case of a Ten of Swords in the future, she might not be able to avoid the defeat, particularly if the competition or combat is already in play. But with the Hanged Man reversed, laziness is a decision, so I can tell the querent that she *might* be lazy, or "it looks like" she will. Based on one card, I don't even know if laziness is the wrong decision for her. If the Hanged Man reversed in the future follows a Ten of Swords in the present, she might not be strong enough to handle the hard work, and taking an easier path might be the smartest possible decision, based on the wounds she's currently experiencing.

Another way of looking at Past-Present-Future is as an unfolding, an act of becoming:

> *The past, which was [card], became the present, which is [card]; next, it will become [future card].*

One reason I always use layouts in which the present, or the querent, or the situation, is in the center is because everything emanates from it, in all directions. There are two directions in this simple reading, but I like to keep that emanation-from-the-center principle in every reading.

If a querent doesn't like the future, he can change the present, because the future is emanating from the present. If the querent doesn't understand the present, look for causality in the past. If the querent understands a decision he made in the past, he's better able to change that decision, which impacts the present and the future.

Let's keep going with our examples:

Past: Ten of Swords/Present: Nine of Wands/Future: Seven of Swords: *In the past, you were defeated, <u>and therefore</u>, you are now guarded, cautious, and distrustful. It's a good thing you're so guarded, because the future brings a theft or deception, perhaps from the same source that wounded you in the past.*

Past: Ten of Swords/Present: Nine of Wands/Future: Five of Cups: *In the past, you were defeated, <u>and therefore</u>, you are now guarded, cautious, and distrustful. The future shows a deep sense of loss, disproportionate to the actual loss. The Five of Cups is someone grieving over a loss even though the person still has plenty—your guardedness today may be distorting your vision, and this <u>looks like</u> it will cause you pain in the future.*

Here are two different future cards that completely change the meaning of the present card. If the future needs to be guarded against, then a cautious card in the present makes sense and is positive. If the future brings emotional pain, then perhaps the root of that pain is in the present or the past, and it's time to unravel the thread of defeat that leads to that future.

Note also that it makes sense to relate the Seven of Swords to the Ten of Swords, and not just because they are the same suit (and therefore a pattern). The future and the past are connected. You can expect a relationship among all the cards, especially in a small reading.

Changing the Time Sequence

What if you want a time sequence that isn't past-present-future, or is more specific than just past-present-future? The simple answer is to declare in advance what the reading will be, and then stick to that.

Here are some examples:

- Yesterday-Today-Tomorrow
- January-February-March
- Yesterday-Next Month-Six Months from Now

It's important, though, not to revert to a more nebulous "past" if the card doesn't immediately resemble what actually happened yesterday. Readings like this can be stressful for the Psychic Child, who awaits the moment when you doubt her. When your timeline is specific, there's room to doubt, and that can be nerve-wracking.

Instead, be firm. Be committed to the fact that your chosen meanings *are* the meanings of these positions, and you'll find that you'll be able to work within those parameters.

Of course, you may find it simpler to tweak the layout, so that January-February-March looks different from Past-Present-Future. For example, you could do something as simple as using a straight line of three cards (as in illustration 18) when you mean Past-Present-Future, while using a fanned layout when you mean months, or vice versa. Or you could imagine months as being in the positions of the twelve numbers on a clock, and place "month" cards in the correct spot of the circular clock face you are visualizing: 1, 2, 3 for January-February-March.

Influences Layout

Note that if you use a significator in this layout, it goes in position 1, and then the first card is placed directly on top of it.

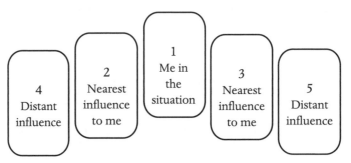

Illustration 19: Influences Layout

This snapshot layout answers the question "What is going on around me?" (with "me" being the querent). I used a variation on this for the court cards reading in chapter 3 (illustration 15).

An influence, in this layout, can be a person, a memory, a relationship, a job—it's a very open-ended word. Sometimes I vary this layout by using the principle that the left side is the unconscious and the right side is the conscious, so cards 2 and 4 are influences the querent is not aware of, while cards 3 and 5 are influences the querent already knows about.

This is also a simple layout in terms of seeing how a card's meaning will change according to its position. Remember that when you study card meanings from any book or guide, you're learning them *as if they are the central card.* Virtually every meaning in any book you study will fit well in position 1 in the Influences layout, but you're going to be shifting the meanings of the other four cards.

Sample Reading: Influences Layout

The following is a reading I did for someone "blind," which is to say, she didn't tell me her question until after the reading was over (illustration 20).

King of Wands *Four of Pentacles* *The Chariot* *Justice reversed* *The Star*

Illustration 20: Influences Reading (Robin Wood Tarot)

Before I began reading the cards, I noticed a pattern and said to the querent that the presence of three majors indicated the reading was very important to her and involved her understanding of who she was as a person. She agreed.

Position 1: *Me in the situation*

Chariot: *Control, mastery, the need to maintain strict control to prevent chaos.*

Chariot in Position 1: *The question is about your ability to control the situation; you feel you have to hold on tight and work very hard or chaos will ensue.* Notice how similar this is to the meaning of the card.

Position 2: *Nearest influence you don't know about*

Four of Pentacles: *Miserliness; greed; grasping tightly to what you have and failing to see that you could have more.*

Four of Pentacles in Position 2: *A greedy person or institution is the biggest hidden influence on your need to maintain control, or it's your own short-sighted attitude that is the hidden influence.*

Here, I advocated for the hidden influence being a subconscious attitude, while my querent was sure it was an outside party. I felt like the outside party wasn't a *hidden* influence, since she was well aware of it, and thus we were talking about a subconscious attitude—the card represented the way she was holding tightly to the Chariot's reins, and was telling her that she wasn't seeing outside opportunities as a result. She disagreed.

Position 3: *Nearest influence you are aware of*

Justice Reversed: *Injustice.*

Justice Reversed in Position 3: *You've been screwed. You're not being treated fairly. The reason you have to struggle so hard is because of the way you're being treated.*

Here, we're certain that it's an outside party that is committing the injustice. If the card was in position 1, it might have been the querent committing the injustice, or it might have been that the question was about a legal concern or about the injustice itself.

Position 4: *Distant influence you may not know about*

King of Wands: *A powerful man connected to wand concerns (building, establishing, working, creating).*

King of Wands in Position 4: *There is a powerful man pulling strings and advocating for you, helping you through this situation. He's not a money guy—he's not someone in finance or payroll; he's related specifically to your work.*

Position 5: *Distant influence you're aware of*

The Star: *Physical, psychological, and spiritual well-being; health; balance.*

The Star in Position 5: *Maintaining your health and well-being is important in order to keep going. The situation requires strength, energy, and focus. If anything happens to your health, you won't be able to keep going, and this is a concern of yours. You can see that the Chariot's intensity requires the support of the Star.*

After the reading was finished, the querent told me the question was about work. She is an adjunct professor and is angry about institutional greed that prevents her and her colleagues from being well-paid or advancing in their careers. She carries a heavy course load that can be exhausting. She has a dean she is friendly with, whom she has long suspected of pulling strings behind the scenes to make sure she has enough classes to support herself.

Let's think about what this sample reading taught us about reading a card based on its position. Position 1 was the situation/question/querent in the context of the question. It is "me as I ask this question." Every oth~~-- --~~rd is an influence and therefore secondary. Every other card must refer back to the first card.

The grasping quality of the Four of Pentacles thus relates back to the Charioteer's grip on the reins. The King of Wands is an advocate who helps the querent maintain control of the reins. Justice reversed is the reason the querent has to struggle so hard, and the Star is necessary to continue the struggle. Every secondary card is read in relation to the central card. You can say that secondary cards interact with the primary card, just as you can say that a card interacts with its position in the layout.

Exercise: Relating Cards to One Another

In the previous reading, I stated: "Every other card must refer back to the first card." This exercise is your opportunity to work on that, using the same Influences spread. You can do this reading for yourself or a willing friend. Read out loud even if you are alone.

1. If you are using a significator, pull it from the deck and place it before you.

2. Then begin with several deep, cleansing breaths, and center yourself.

3. If you are alone, ask your question out loud. If you are reading for someone else, allow them to choose whether they will ask a question out loud or keep it private.

4. Shuffle the cards until you feel it's time to stop.

5. If you are reading for a querent, let the querent shuffle also.

6. Lay out five cards as shown in illustration 19.

7. Look for patterns first, sharing anything you see with the querent (or reading out loud if alone).

8. Read card 1: Me in the situation.

9. Read cards 2 through 5. Each card should be related back to card 1. Your task is not to remember the meaning of each card—you should already know that. Your task, instead, is to interpret each card as if it is secondary to card 1: What is card 2's relationship to card 1? What is card 3's relationship to card 1? And so on.

10. Draw your conclusion. How does finding a conclusion help relate cards 2 through 5 back to card 1, to tell a single story?

11. Record your results in your journal.

CELTIC CROSS LAYOUT

The Celtic Cross layout is the most familiar and wide-ranging snapshot spread, and it's the one most tarot readers learn first (illustration 21). Almost every book on the tarot has a variation on the Celtic Cross.

Keep in mind that there are many variations of this spread! From the order in which the "cross" portion of the reading is laid down to the meanings of individual card positions (especially in the "arm" portion), you'll find numerous authors contradicting one another. Our focus here is on the interaction of a card with its position, so if you've learned a different version of this layout that you prefer, the lesson will still be of value.

Traditionally, the Celtic Cross is always laid out with a significator, which is placed beneath card 1 before the shuffle.

Position 1: Covering (the significator)—This is the situation, which is so closely aligned with the querent that it completely covers her. (This is why a significator is important in this spread. The entire reading will take place as if the querent *is* the significator and the cards surround her.)

Position 2: Crossing—This is what crosses the querent, what works against her interests, specifically in regard to card 1. The crossing card is always read as if reversed.

Position 3: Above—Known as the "crown" card, this is variously read as the goal, the best possible outcome, or the possible future (the future following card 10).

Position 4: Below—Known as the "foundation" card, this is the reality that the querent stands upon. It's not the situation or the question, it's the unquestioned background—like water to a fish.

Position 5: Behind—The recent past; this is anything that has happened in the past one to three weeks, and/or anything with a fading influence.

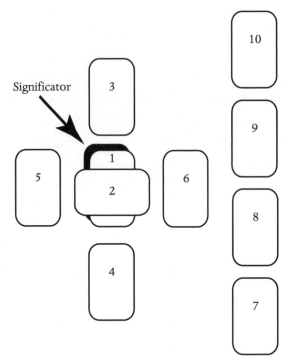

Illustration 21: Celtic Cross Layout

Position 6: Ahead—The near future; this is a prediction of something that will happen in the next few days.

Position 7: Environment—The people and things around the querent, including family, living companions, coworkers, job conditions, and so on. It's not the querent and should never be interpreted as the querent's inner life.

Position 8: Self-Image—Who the querent thinks she is.

Position 9: Hopes and Fears—This is a purely psychological card and should not be mistaken for a prediction or a description of how things really are.

Position 10: Outcome—This card answers the question. If there wasn't a question, it indicates what the current actions will lead to. It adds up the past (card 5), present (cards 1, 2, and 4), future (card 6), and other conditions surrounding the querent (cards 7, 8, and 9), and says what the result will be if nothing is changed.

Let's take a card—the Two of Pentacles (illustration 22)—and imagine it in each position. I'll write up each position as if I'm describing the card to a querent. Pay attention to the way that the card stays the same and yet changes as a result of moving from place to place.

Illustration 22: Two of Pentacles (Robin Wood Tarot)

Two of Pentacles: *Keeping things in balance. The juggler keeps things in balance by keeping his balls in the air.*

Position 1: *Covering—Your overriding concern right now is maintaining balance, keeping all your balls in the air. Right now you're fine, and your focus is on making sure you stay fine.*

Position 2: *Crossing—Keeping balanced in the face of all the factors in your life is the thing that makes [meaning of card 1] harder. Staying in balance and keeping all these balls in the air works at cross-purposes to [card 1].*

Position 3: *Above—Your goal is to be in balance and to be able to manage all the facets of your life without apparent effort.*

Position 4: *Below—Here we see that your life is all about staying in balance. As you [reference back to card 1], your foundation is the effort to stay in balance.*

The foundation card (position 4) might not make a lot of sense without referring to other cards, so I laid out three cards to give us a covering, crossing, and goal card (illustration 23).

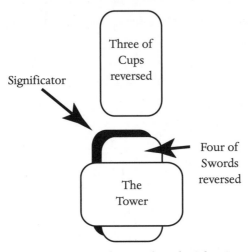

Illustration 23: First Three Cards in the Celtic Cross

Now we can read a foundation Two of Pentacles as follows:

Here we see that the foundation of your life is about staying in balance and also about juggling many things. The period of rest and reclusion you're coming out of [Four of Swords reversed] must have seemed really unnatural and awkward to someone who is used to keeping many balls in the air. Fortunately, you are still that person and can draw on those abilities as you regain your bearings.

The Four of Swords reversed covers; the querent is coming to the end of a long rest, illness, or period of isolation. The Tower crosses; a disaster of some kind forces an end to exile, or perhaps the disaster is what pushes the querent out of exile—the other cards will tell the tale. The important thing is that the foundation card teaches us something of who the querent is: whatever the disaster, whatever the current period of rest and recovery, this is someone for whom balance and busyness are normal.

Suppose the Tower and the Four of Swords reversed were switched, with the Tower covering and the Four crossing. Then our interpretation would be something like this:

Here we see that the foundation of your life is about staying in balance and also about juggling many things. The disaster that has ripped through your life [Tower] is something that you have an ability to overcome—your foundation shows us that. The desire to get away from the stress and chaos and take a breather [Four of Swords reversed] won't help you, but the balance and agility required to keep many balls in the air is exactly what you need.

Since the need for rest, repose, and contemplation (Four of Swords reversed) crosses the querent, we can assume it's doing her no good. Her foundation here represents core inner qualities that can help her.

Position 5: *Behind—You used to be really good at keeping things in balance.*

This is an okay reading of the card in this position, but it's kind of a "general past" interpretation. The Celtic Cross benefits from keeping very specifically to the stated meaning of each position. "Behind" is the immediate past, an event that happened or a person encountered. Here is a better reading:

In the recent past, there was a spate of responsibilities that forced you to stay on your toes and really juggle things, yet you were able to stay in balance.

Position 6: *Ahead—You're going to be called on to do a real balancing act in the next few days. Perhaps some extra responsibilities will be handed to you.*

This is the obvious meaning, but sometimes this position in particular is a place where you can be really intuitive. Maybe the querent is going to meet an acrobat or a circus performer!

Position 7: *Environment—The people around you are really balancing a lot of things right now.*

Other cards will indicate why this is important. Perhaps the people around her are unavailable to be supportive of the querent. Perhaps the querent has always wished she could be as good at staying balanced as her coworkers or family seem to be. Perhaps she's working in a general atmosphere of controlled stress. Look to the other cards to flesh this out. We'll learn more about this in the next chapter.

Position 8: *Self-Image—You see yourself as someone who is always handling a dozen things at once. You pride yourself on keeping it all together.*

Position 9: *Hopes and Fears—Deep down, you're afraid you can't handle all the things that are being thrown at you. You hope to be seen as serene and in balance, but you're afraid you'll look like a fool and become overwhelmed.*

Position 10: *Outcome—Despite [whatever negative cards are predicted], you'll ultimately be able to handle everything with a sense of balance.* Of course, if there aren't any negative cards, you would read this differently.

The Two of Pentacles changed subtly throughout this reading. It remained itself, but as it interacted with its own position in the layout, the resulting interpretation of the card changed.

At the foundation, we also saw the beginning of how cards interact with one another, which will be the subject of our next chapter.

Decision Layouts

Most of the time these days, I use some sort of decision layout. A good decision reading often has many qualities in common with a snapshot reading; it tells you where you're at now and what you're doing, and contrasts that with an alternative. One of the following readings is "what you're doing" versus "what you should be doing." Another I use takes a different approach: "what will happen if you keep doing what you're doing" versus "what will happen if you make a change." These layouts work because most of the time when people are struggling to make a decision, they're already inclined in one direction, and their behavior is already leading them somewhere. They just need to be told whether that's the right direction.

Yes/No Layout

The simplest Yes/No layout is simply to shuffle and cut the deck, looking at the cut card. Upright is "yes" and reversed is "no." You can use this for straightforward questions: *Will my meeting start on schedule? Should we go to the movies tonight?* Things where you don't really need to read more meaning into the answer.

For a more nuanced Yes/No reading, I use the following six-card layout all the time (illustration 24). I first learned it from Eden Gray, and by now it's second nature to me. It's simple, it's fast, it's accurate, and it's easy.

For this layout, don't use a significator.

Shuffle the deck as usual, making sure to get those reversals in there. Cut three piles, from left to right. Flip over the top card of each pile and place above the pile. Those are your first three cards. Then flip over each pile so that the bottom card is face up. Now you have six cards. (It doesn't matter if you flip a card/pile from bottom to top or sideways, as long as you always do it the same way.)

Now count the reversals. More upright and the answer is yes. More reversed and the answer is no. Three of each means the question cannot be answered at this time.

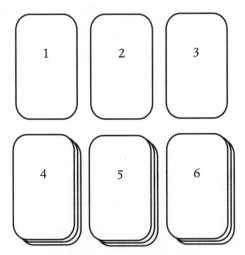

Illustration 24: Yes/No Layout

Now you can read the cards as in the Past-Present-Future layout (illustration 17). There are two cards for each position: positions 1 and 4 are the past, 2 and 5 are the present, and 3 and 6 are the future. They will *explain* the yes-or-no answer, but no matter what information you get from the cards, the yes or no is based on reversals only.

I find this layout refreshing. It lets me read a lot about the past, present, and future without letting the querent say, "But doesn't that mean I should really...?" Remember that a querent is already leaning one way or the other, and is looking for you to confirm what they want to hear. Sometimes you just can't do that.

Reading in Sequence

We've seen three layouts so far in which the past, present, and future are read from left to right: this one (Yes/No), the three-card Past-Present-Future, and the Celtic Cross. Unless you read one of a handful of languages such as Hebrew, your eye naturally sequences information from left to right, because that's the way you read.

Read layouts in sequence from left to right to allow your brain to process information in a way that seems natural. The sequence of events you see naturally, and the sequence of events that the layout describes, should match. If you invent your own layout or revise one you've found here or elsewhere, keep this in mind.

Also keep in mind that cards will tend to take this sequence even when there's no explicit past-present-future in the reading.

In chapter 3, we looked at a sample reading for court cards (illustration 15). The layout used was a seven-card version of the Influences layout (illustration 19). The difference was, I put two cards in each of the "distant influence" positions. This gave a fuller spread of environmental concerns. With two cards side by side, even though there was nothing in the layout about time sequence, I naturally read them in sequence, so that the Two of Wands in that reading came before, and perhaps caused, the Knight of Pentacles reversed.

Another sequence the eye naturally understands is "above" and "below." The Celtic Cross layout does a wonderful job of making this explicit; the querent seems to stand on the foundation, and the crown seems to be above his head.

When you see two cards one above the other, as you do in each section of the Yes/No layout in illustration 24, you'll naturally see the bottom card as a kind of foundation, and the top card as standing on it, floating above it, or emerging from it. In other words, the bottom card will tend to come first.

In the sample layout in illustration 25, you can see that the answer is a strong yes, since only one card is reversed. What else can we learn?

A pattern emerges: Three court cards indicate that this is a decision involving people, or a situation with a lot of people around, perhaps a social event. Two kings indicate that authority and control are important. The Page and the Six of Cups both depict children/youth.

Remember that this layout differs from the other three-card Past-Present-Future layout in that there are two cards per period of time. In the past, we see waiting. If the Two of Wands was the only past card, we could say, *You were waiting for news about an opportunity*, and then look to the present and future to see how it turned out. Here, though, we see a Page of Pentacles as well. Waiting resulted in an answer about money (pentacles) from a student or young person or school (pages are often students). Since I'm reading for my professor again, this makes perfect sense.

To a certain extent, the meaning of the Page is altered by the fact that it relates to the Two of Wands. Instead of describing the person that the Page is, I describe him or her in relation to the Two. The two cards in each time period have to communicate the message of the reading as a single unit: *these* are the past instead of *this* is the past.

Similarly, the present shows a king on top of the Wheel of Fortune reversed. I see these two cards as being in contradiction to each other: the King is a controlling force, and the Wheel is that card in the deck that tells us that luck will have its way—not everything is under our control. Which is it? At the present moment, the querent doesn't know.

Notice that only the present is uncertain; only the present has both a reversal and an upright card. The querent is uncertain at this moment, even though the past has been secure and the future will be secure.

When two cards in the same position contradict each other, we can perceive that as a mistaken belief: *You think this King is in control, but really it's all up to fate.* Here I interpret the King in the above position to mean he is an idea, while the Wheel below is reality: a foundation is as real as the earth beneath our feet.

Illustration 25: Yes/No Reading (Classic Tarot)

In the future, the Six of Cups comes from the King of Cups. There will be strong emotional satisfaction in the outcome; neither card has that meaning, but the future is 100 percent cups—two cards in two positions. This suggests that emotions will come into play, and with a positive reading like this, that's how I interpret it. The King of Cups brings the querent to a future where happy memories are experienced.

Naturally, the professor was asking about school again, this time about classes that she would or would not be offered. Since she is an adjunct professor, each semester is fraught with stress about whether her schedule will allow her to make a living, and sometimes it's pure luck. Fortunately, her answer and her actual outcome were positive.

Vitruvian Man Layout

This is my single favorite layout. I learned about it in a magazine article over twenty years ago—I don't know who to credit for it—but it is wonderfully simple and rich.

The Vitruvian Man is the Leonardo da Vinci illustration of a man with his arms outstretched (illustration 26). The image seems to form a five-pointed star (a pentagram—not unlike the pentacles suit), as shown in illustration 27.

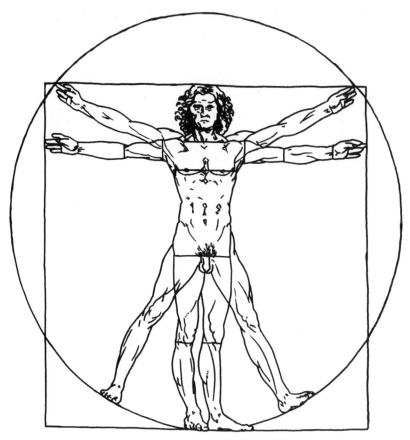

Illustration 26: Vitruvian Man

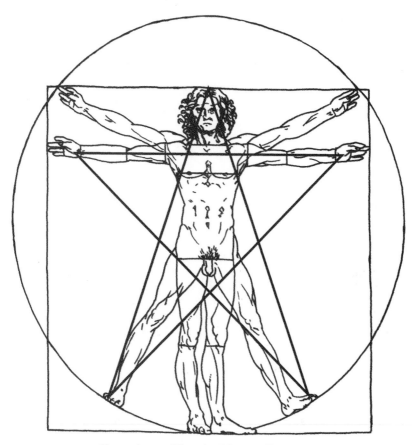

Illustration 27: Vitruvian Man as a Pentagram

The layout of the Vitruvian Man is simple and easy to remember, because it's easy to visualize the human body. The cards are placed as though you are drawing a pentagram, starting at the top (illustration 28).

I learned this reading with two cards in each position, although I often use it for a quick six-card reading. If you do the twelve-card version, lay out the pentagram twice, so that the head is cards 1 and 7, the left foot (always read from your own point of view) is cards 2 and 8, and so on.

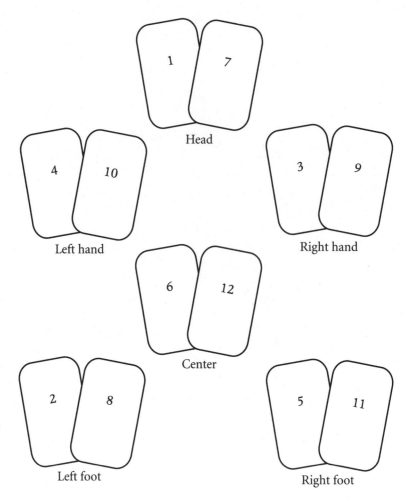

Illustration 28: Vitruvian Man Layout

One thing I love about this spread is the way that snapshot and decision cards are interspersed throughout. It's also a layout that has practical and spiritual components.

Although the cards are initially placed as numbered, I tend to read them from either top to bottom (as in the following example), or left to right (in keeping with the natural sequencing discussed earlier). In any case, I always save the center cards for last.

Position 1/7: Head—Where your head is at. What you're thinking. Your primary concern.

Position 4/10: Left Hand—What you've been doing. "Hands" in this layout indicate action. This position, the left hand from the reader's point of view, is past/present actions.

Position 3/9: Right Hand—What you should be doing. This card is why I classify this as a decision layout. You have the opportunity, as a reader, to see if the two hands are very similar or very different.

Position 2/8: Left Foot—Where you stand. This is basically a foundation card, since it's where the querent stands. But this spread emphasizes movement—the querent moves from this foot to the next, so it's possible to look at how the querent's life has changed in a broad sense. A foundation card in the Celtic Cross is stable, whereas this card is more like a step in life's journey.

Position 5/11: Right Foot—Where you're going. This is the future card. It's important to look at the relationship between the right hand and the right foot—is the querent heading in the direction he should be?

Position 6/12: Center—What Spirit/God/the Gods want you to do. Normally you expect this card to be consistent with the right hand, but every now and then, this position will throw you a curve ball and make you rethink the entire reading. It can be a challenging layout for that reason.

The Vitruvian Man layout gives us the opportunity to see how to work with pairs of cards in a different way. Previously, we've seen side-by-side or top-and-bottom pairs. In this layout, the pairs of cards are placed in a fan.

Sample Vitruvian Man Reading

As usual, we can start the reading by looking for patterns (illustration 29). Sometimes it benefits a reading to wait until you've looked at the individual cards before looking for patterns, and sometimes the meaning of a pattern becomes clearer later in the reading. For the purposes of this book, we look for patterns first, but in real-life readings, you will do it in whatever order feels intuitively correct.

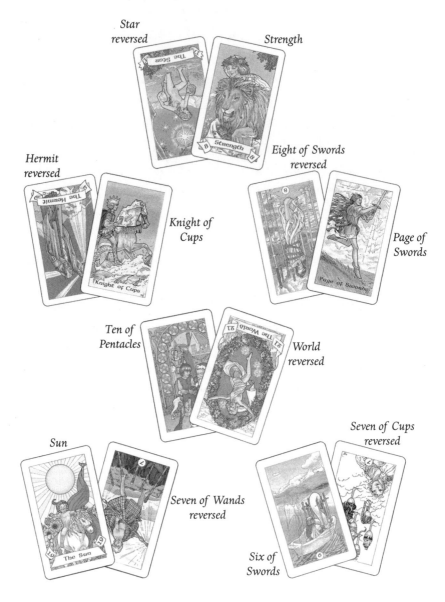

Illustration 29: Vitruvian Man Reading (Robin Wood Tarot)

There are five major arcana in this spread. Our handy Distribution of Cards chart (at the beginning of chapter 3) says that three or four are normal in a twelve-card layout, so this isn't a huge anomaly. What's interesting, though, is that both cards in the head position are majors. This indicates right off the bat that our querent thinks the problem is bigger and more important than it may actually be.

There are two sevens (both reversed) and two eights (including Strength). Any repeated number is statistically notable. Our keyword for seven is "willpower," and for eight it's "progress." As an overview, we see that a lack of willpower on the querent's part is impeding progress.

Position 1/7: Head

Star Reversed: General ill health, in body, mind, or spirit. A health crisis. Disconnection from the self or one's spiritual nature. Pessimism and darkness.

Strength: Compassion. Spiritual strength through love rather than force.

Interpretation: *You're worried about your health and your own dark attitude. You've made an effort to become more compassionate and to bring that compassion into your life.* Usually, when doing a reading, I'll state the meaning of the position as I read each card, so it'll be, *Where your head is at—You're worried about your health …* I do this in each position.

How the Pair Works Together: We know these are huge concerns about life changes because both cards are majors. Because Strength literally overlays the Star reversed, we have reason to suspect that the querent is trying to overlay underlying fears with outward behavior; he's trying to stuff the fears away by being loving and kind and so on.

Position 4/10: Left Hand

Hermit Reversed: This can mean leaving a "hermitage"—after a period of isolation—and reentering the world, or it can mean rejecting the advice of a guru or teacher; refusing to learn.

Knight of Cups: A man bringing love or a loving message into life. A Prince Charming.

Interpretation: *You've ended a period of isolating yourself. You're working on getting out into the world in a way that is loving and friendly.*

How the Pair Works Together: The Knight of Cups allowed me to reject the "refusing to learn" option for the Hermit reversed; the reading in general is already clearly about the querent's efforts to engage more with the world in a loving way. *Get out of your dark, dreary head and love humanity* can be a phrase that applies to both the head and left hand. We can understand now that the querent isn't just thinking about engaging more compassionately, but is actively doing so. The Knight is a result of the Hermit. Notice that in a fan pairing (as opposed to two cards side by side), we see that the top card partially obscures the bottom card. In this case, the Knight covers the Hermit's lamp. If we think of the Hermit as someone isolated, and his lamp as his wisdom or teaching, then the Knight's placement supports the notion that we should discuss isolation (and its end) rather than see the Hermit as a teacher.

Position 2/8: Left Foot. Knowing this querent, and seeing what the cards had to offer, I wanted to make sure we thoroughly discussed past and present before we got into advice and future.

Sun: A happy child leaves the garden. Venturing out into the unknown, with joy and positivity. The present situation is safe and comfortable but childlike; the card indicates a willingness to move beyond the safe walls of childhood and venture into adulthood. Joy is within.

Seven of Wands Reversed: A failure to plan; the querent hasn't taken high ground and is unprepared. The Seven of Wands shows a conflict in which the querent has high ground and will win; reversed, he has failed to prepare and is overwhelmed.

Interpretation: *The Sun tells me that you're ready to leave your garden. You're fine and happy as a sheltered child, but you're ready to grow up and venture out into the world, and that's what your life has been about. You've made some real mistakes and you haven't been prepared for the real world, and this has been a cause of some pain to you. Maybe the Seven of Wands* *reversed here is why you've got the Star reversed on your mind.* It's helpful, throughout a reading, to refer back to cards you've already read.

How the Pair Works Together: The Sun is working marvelously with the Hermit to affirm that the querent is expanding his life. The Hermit moves from isolation to connection, with the Knight of Cups forming loving connections (not necessarily romances), while the Sun moves from safety to the unknown. It looks like the first thing that has happened to the querent in this journey is that he's gotten his ass kicked.

Just as the Knight obscured the Hermit's lamp, here the Seven of Wands obscures the Sun's victory banner: this tells us that the journey (the child on horseback) is important, but the success of the journey is not visible.

The querent has recently moved from his family home into his own apartment. He's struggling financially. We see, though, that the struggle is less about money (there is only one pentacle in the reading) and more about connecting to the world.

When we get to the final cards, we'll see that the querent struggles between an idealized life and a practical one. We can see the seeds of that with these two cards: the Sun is an idealized version of moving out, while the Seven brings the querent down to earth rapidly.

Position 3/9: Right Hand

Eight of Swords Reversed: The end of an illness or an abusive situation. Getting your sea legs back after an illness can be difficult. Release from fear or imprisonment.

Page of Swords: An agile young person. A dancer. A student of ideas, language, or dance. This card can also mean glibness, deception, or dishonesty.

Interpretation: *The Eight of Swords seems to relate to both the Hermit and the Seven of Wands: You should be gentle with yourself. Your isolated period at your "hermitage" has left you a little weak, and you will naturally make* *mistakes. You should be strengthening your body as a way of strengthening your spirit. The Page of Swords suggests that physical activity will help move you toward the future you want.* Here I took advantage of prior knowledge of the querent—since I knew he was considering taking dance classes, this card seemed like a direct reference to that. I've referred to the Page of Swords as the tarot's dancer for years, and here it was, in the "should be doing" position, suggesting that dance would help the querent.

How the Pair Works Together: The Page seems to suggest a solution to the problem of the Eight. They're both swords, indicating, in this case, movement. (Recall from chapter 3 that a pattern of swords indicates that the reading has a lot to do with aggression, conflict, speech, or argument, or that there is intense movement related to the reading.) Among the swords, these card aren't particularly aggressive, violent, or conflict-oriented, and neither is the Six of Swords (position 5), the third sword in the reading. I think movement and change are the order of the day. The seven/eight pattern of this reading can be defined as "a lack of willpower impedes progress." We've already learned a lot about the goals of this reading—movement away from isolation and out into the world, growing up, managing practical life better, and feeling less dark. Here we learn two things: the querent should be forgiving of his own flaws, just as a recently released prisoner should be expected to have a period of adjustment, and the querent should use physical activity, specifically dance, to feel more connected to the real world. My intuition tells me that physical movement will act on a non-physical level to help move the querent forward in all sorts of ways.

Position 5/11: Right Foot

Six of Swords: A journey away from sorrow.

Seven of Cups Reversed: Paralysis. Inability to make a decision.

Interpretation: *Your journey is stalled by your inability to decide. It's crucial that you make a decision—any decision—rather than stay paralyzed.* Since the querent works in the tourism industry, I suggested that the Six of

Swords—a card of travel—might represent his job, and his paralysis might be related to career.

How the Pair Works Together: With just the Six of Swords, a normal interpretation would be that the querent was about to take a journey or was planning a trip of some kind. However, paired with a card of indecision and paralysis, this seemed unlikely. When the two cards were read together, it seemed like a narrative about a delayed trip or an inability to choose what trip to take. The way the two cards are laid out, you can't even see the journey, so I focused the reading on indecision. The seven pattern also indicated that this was the more important card.

Position 6/12: What Spirit wants you to do

Ten of Pentacles: All good things; a happy home, wealth, a loving family. Can also mean an inheritance or a family reunion.

World Reversed: Loss of possessions, both material and spiritual. Loss of position or rank. Can also be the refusal to learn lessons from life.

Interpretation: Here I was faced with a situation that is a huge challenge for many tarot readers: What do you do when a negative card appears in a positive position? If there's something dark, unpleasant, or disastrous in a position designated as "what you should do" or "goal" or something like that, it can be challenging and confusing for both the reader and the querent. This is where understanding that the card and the position are *interactive* is vital. In this case, the interaction of the will of the Gods with a negative card was saying, *Don't do that. Do this instead.* By the way, if you're reading for someone who knows anything about the tarot, it's helpful to draw attention to the conflict—the querent is already noticing it and worrying about it.

This position is what Spirit or the Gods want you to do. You're probably wondering how the World reversed can possibly be what Spirit wants for you! But look at it next to the Ten of Pentacles. There's all the good things in the world versus the World. Spirit is telling you to ground yourself in the reality of the minor arcana, rather than seeking after some fantastical version of perfect fulfillment. This brings us back to the beginning of the reading—the major arcana in the head position. Your thinking is all about big, important, world-shattering things, and you're asking yourself to be perfect and amazing. What God wants of you is just to live a life—a happy, fulfilling life with family, children, and comfort. The cards here say to let go of seeking after the extraordinary, because it's blinding you to how wonderful the ordinary can be.

Look at the Eight of Swords reversed. The advice of this card is to be gentle and forgiving of yourself. You need that advice because of these grandiose ideas you have about how awesome you're supposed to be. See how it relates back to letting go of the World (which is the World reversed). The World card is as grandiose as anything in the deck—and Spirit says that's not what your goal should be right now. Your goal should be the Ten of Pentacles.

There's a lot more to say about this reading. We'll be revisiting it and some other readings in the next chapter.

Expanding Upon a Layout

There are two ways I've expanded a layout: by design (planned in advance) and spontaneously (in the moment).

Dropping Cards

Sometimes, during the course of a reading, you want more information about a particular card or position. Sometimes you as the reader, or the querent, will simply not *get* the meaning of a card. It doesn't relate to the querent's life, or you can't seem to make it flow with the rest of the reading. In truth, it may be disconnected from the rest of the reading— another part of the querent's life making an appearance and having an unexpected influence on the primary concern. Often, a court card confuses a querent; you as a reader may be certain that this is a specific person, but the querent can't figure out who you're talking about.

If you find yourself in this situation, take the next card in the deck and place it (drop it) over the top of the card in question. Read it as a single card, which is answering the question "What does [the original card] mean?"

Whenever you add a card to a reading, just keep dealing as if the card were part of the original layout. Don't reshuffle or cut the cards.

Adding a Three-Card Fan of Past-Present-Future

Another way to expand on a reading is to add a three-card fan of Past-Present-Future to the bottom of a reading. This adds a kind of overview, and can wrap up a reading. If you have a sit-down appointment with a querent, it can be a great way of finishing—a kind of cherry on top of the spread.

Illustration 30 shows a three-card fan of Past-Present-Future added to the bottom of a Celtic Cross. The fan helps to sum up the basic trajectory of the reading and can provide supportive cards for anything the querent still questions.

Read an added three-card fan as if it has been part of the layout all along. Note if it is consistent with patterns that already existed in the layout, or if it adds a pattern you hadn't seen before. In chapter 5, we will learn about cards interacting with other cards. You'll find that these added cards can interact with the rest of the layout.

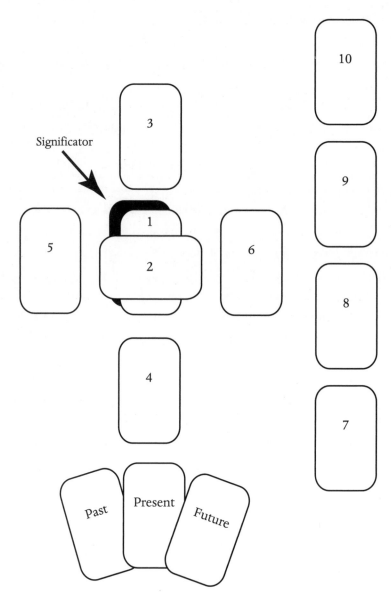

Illustration 30: Celtic Cross with Three-Card Fan of Past-Present-Future

Making a Card a Significator

Sometimes a single card in a spread takes on great meaning. In the introduction, I describe how this happened during the very first tarot reading I received. Susan used a Celtic Cross layout, and we dug deeply into what was going on in my life at the time. One card was clearly my husband, whom I'd left just weeks before. I needed to know what was going on with him.

She pulled the card that represented him out of the layout, left it on the table, shuffled the rest of the cards, and made his card the significator. Now we were reading *his* cards.

This technique is, again, best suited to a longer consultation. I've spent years honing my skills at psychic fairs and public events where a line forms and you're best served by streamlined readings. But I've also had a number of clients, over the years, with whom I do in-depth readings taking an hour or more. Here we can dive deeply into multiple aspects of a querent's life, and here is where this technique can be really powerful.

Although it's traditional to use a court card for a significator, you can pull any card, and read people, situations, jobs, relationships … whatever the cards dictate.

Expanding the Planned Layout

Dropping a card, adding a three-card fan, or pulling a card as a significator are all techniques that can be used spontaneously, in the moment of the reading. You can also expand standard readings as a matter of course.

In chapter 3, the five-card Influences layout was expanded to seven cards by adding one card to each of the distant influences positions (illustration 15). This layout could easily be expanded to nine cards by adding to the near influences in the same way. In fact, a three-card fan could be added to each of the influences positions, although you might choose a different technique for position 1. You certainly could put two or three cards there, but you might also choose to single out "me in the situation" in some way.

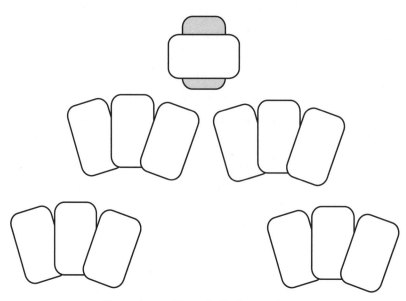

Illustration 31: Expanded Influences Layout

Here is an example. This is essentially the same Influences layout as shown in illustration 19. Positions 2 through 5 have been expanded to three-card fans in each case. Position 1 has been expanded to a cross, which you would read the same way you read it in the Celtic Cross layout: covering and crossing—in other words, "me in the situation" and "that which is working against me."

A lot of people invent their own layouts, and that's great, but you might find it easier to be creative with an existing layout, tweaking it to make it your own, rather than starting from scratch.

Expanded Celtic Cross Layout

In 1982, Susan introduced me to Lorraine, who she told me was the single best tarot reader she knew. I have long since lost touch with Lorraine (she was always Susan's friend and not really mine), but I learned a great deal from her.

Lorraine's expanded Celtic Cross was my go-to layout for many years (illustration 32). Using it taught me a great deal about the tarot (including a lot of the material in chapter 5). It's a deep, twenty-four-card dive into the issues facing the querent.

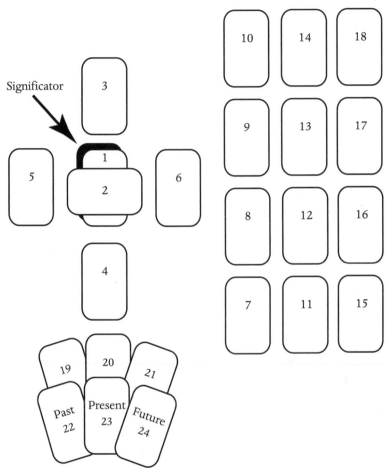

Illustration 32: Expanded Celtic Cross Layout

There are a couple different ways of setting up this layout:

- Lay out each card one at a time, announcing its meaning and giving a brief interpretation: *This covers you...* When the first eighteen cards have been laid out, go back and read everything thoroughly, looking at patterns and other interactions. Leave the last six cards

for the end, after all other reading is done, just as if you were dropping a three-card fan on any other reading.

- Lay out the first ten cards as just described, and then add eleven
  through eighteen before continuing with your interpretation. Lay
  out the last six cards in the same manner as before.

- Lay out everything and then read.

In this spread, cards 7, 11, and 15 all represent the environment. The
same goes for each set of three—they are all read with the same meaning: self-image (8, 12, 16), hopes and fears (9, 13, 17), and outcome (10,
14, 18). In the bottom fan, 19 and 22 are both the past, 20 and 23 are
both the present, and 21 and 24 are both the future.

Designing Your Own Layout

Many people design their own spreads. Experience with a variety of
layouts will give you a lot of information about what you do and don't
like in a tarot spread, and may inspire you to create one or more spreads
specifically suited to your needs, your personal style, and the types of
readings you do. For example, I've stated that I find the Celtic Cross
best for long, intimate consultations, whereas most of my clients these
days prefer short readings. This means that if I were in the process of
creating my own spread, it would be shorter. I also travel a lot and find
myself doing readings in small corners on the fly, so I'm attracted to
compact readings that don't take up much physical space. Your needs
may be entirely different.

Why create your own tarot layout?

- You have a unique circumstance for which you don't know an existing layout.

- The same questions—yours or the querent's—keep coming up in
  readings and you don't have a satisfying go-to place in a layout to
  seek an answer.

- You think there's an essential component to certain readings or readings in general that layouts you know don't address.

- You think there are nonessential components—unnecessary cards—that layouts you know always seem to include.

One obvious takeaway from this list is that you need a certain amount of experience as a reader to create your own layout. It's easy to think you know what will work, but real-world experience is a better teacher. On the other hand, there's no harm in creating a layout that turns out to be impractical or not something you end up using. The experiment itself can be a rich source of learning.

If you've been doing the homework in this book, you already have a journal of readings that you've done. Go through the journal and see if anything jumps out at you as a gap that could be filled with a modified or brand-new layout. Start jotting down such gaps when you experience them. Start noting questions that come up that don't seem obviously answered by the layout(s) you're using. These preliminary journaling steps will help prepare you for exercise 2 at the end of this chapter.

Some people have one or a few go-to spreads, and some have a huge repertoire. Personally, I've presented in this chapter almost all of the layouts I regularly use. I don't feel the need for more, and even when I teach myself new layouts, I tend to default back to the familiar. I'm the kind of person whose psychic work is enhanced by routine—one less thing to think about, one less thing to disrupt my Psychic Child. Your Psychic Child may be very different, and may be delighted by learning new things and having new psychic toys with which to play.

Homework

Homework Questions

1. Under what circumstances do you choose between "but now" and "and therefore"?

2. What are examples of a good use for each?

3. Under what circumstances do you choose between "and therefore" and "watch out for"?

4. What are examples of a good use for each?

5. Write down ways in which a negative card could be interpreted in a positive position. If the position is "what you should do" and the card has a negative meaning, what are some possible interpretations?

6. What are some circumstances under which you might drop a card on another card?

Homework Answers

1. These are two different ways of transitioning from a past card to a present card.

2. You should be able to come up with examples of a past card and a present card that seem to follow naturally for "and therefore," and two that seem to contradict each another for "but now."

3. These are two different ways of transitioning from a present card to a future card.

4. You should be able to come up with examples of a present card and a future card that seem to follow naturally for "and therefore." You should be able to come up with an example of the future card taking a turn for the worse for "watch out for."

5. There are many possible answers. In the sample Vitruvian Man reading, I offered one: that the negative card is a message about what not to do.

Another possibility is that the querent should just let the negative situation happen, for whatever reason. Suppose "what you should do" is the Nine of Swords (depression, grief). It may be that the querent needs to feel his darkest feelings, really experience them, instead of acting like everything is fine. The message may be that grief will be cleansing.

What answers did you come up with?

6. Possibilities include: You don't fully understand the card's meaning in the reading. The card seems like an outlier; it doesn't connect to the rest of the reading. The querent has additional questions about the card that could best be answered by another card.

Exercises

Exercise 1: Past-Present-Future

This exercise will guide you through a simple Past-Present-Future reading using the connective terms that create interrelationship within the layout. You can do this reading for yourself or a willing friend. Read out loud even if you are alone.

1. Begin with several deep, cleansing breaths, and center yourself.

2. Ask your question out loud. Again, this can be a very simple question, such as "How will my day go tomorrow?"

3. Shuffle the cards until you feel it's time to stop.

4. Lay out three cards as shown in Illustration 18: Renaming Past-Present-Future.

5. Look for patterns first. You will get an immediate sense of the answer to your question by the number of reversals. With only three cards, there's little that can be called statistically normal or abnormal, but you should make note of the distributions anyway.

6. Read the card for the past.

7. Look at the card for the present: does "and therefore" or "but now" apply to it? Say the connective phrase out loud: *In the past, XYZ,* <u>but now,</u> *ABC.*

8. Read the card for the future. Again, determine the correct connective phrase, and say it out loud.

9. Draw your conclusion. See what happens when all three cards lead to a single conclusion. Does it cause you to find more information from the past and present when you have found a conclusion about the future?

10. Record your results in your journal.

11. Repeat this exercise daily until you feel confident that you can easily see the connections between past, present, and future.

Exercise 2: Create a Layout

1. Review the notes in your journal. What questions that querents have asked stand out? What circumstances have you read under that didn't fit an existing layout? Take notes on your answers to these questions.

2. Also note what type of layout this should be: snapshot, decision, or whole life, and the approximate size (number of cards) you're comfortable with.

3. With the answers to steps 1 and 2 in hand, write a short sentence that answers the question "What do you want this layout to do?"

   Examples: (a) I want a whole-life layout that focuses specifically on family relationships; (b) I want a snapshot layout that includes cards for karma or past lives; (c) I want a quick decision reading that isn't Yes/No.

4. This step is actually its own exercise. You should begin with some deep breathing and relaxation. You may even want to use this step as the subject of a meditation.

   Say the sentence you came up with in step 3 to yourself, and allow images, metaphors, or objects to come into your mind that relate to that sentence. For example, the image/metaphor of the Vitruvian Man layout is the human body: the snapshot is based on the head, hands, feet, and center of a person. Your image can be anything, from a tree to a circus to a kitchen table.

5. Next, make a list of position meanings that you like. Don't try to narrow it down yet; just brainstorm on paper.

6. Look at your list from step 5 and eliminate redundant meanings. Is the list now a good size for a single reading, or is it overwhelming? Continue to reduce the list until it feels right.

7. At the same time, consider how these position meanings might fit into the image you selected in step 4. For example, the meaning "current attitude" becomes "where my head is at" in the Vitruvian Man layout. If you are attracted to the image of a house as your layout, then a card representing the subconscious could be the bedroom (where you sleep and dream).

8. Now you have a purpose for your layout, a list of potential position meanings, and an image. It's time to organize your layout. First, set up a rough layout based on your image. Then place individual cards/meanings, keeping in mind the natural sequencing from left to right and bottom to top. When you have a rough layout, record it in your journal.

9. Do a test reading with this rough layout. You may move cards, add cards, add more than one card to one or more meanings/positions, eliminate cards, and so on. You may even discard or change your image as you continue to do test readings and fine-tune the layout.

10. Give your spread a memorable name so you can recall it easily. Enter the final version in your journal.

FIVE

Interactions Between and Among Cards

The next type of interaction we're going to explore is, for me, one of the most rewarding, and often the one I spend the most time on when doing a reading. This is how the cards interact with one another.

We saw the beginnings of this concept in chapter 4. Interacting with layout happens, in part, one card at a time. But we also saw how pairs of cards can interact through an intersection of meaning: cards are read in sequence, so that two cards in the same, shared position can shift meaning depending upon the order in which they appear, and depending upon whether that position places them side by side, above and below, or fanned. Now we're going beyond that.

It's possible to experience the cards as active and alive, as if you are watching a scene laid out before you, with people, landscapes, and action. The people look at or away from each other; they move toward each other or in opposite directions.

Two-Card Interactions

A single line in *Mastering the Tarot* had an enormous influence on me. Eden Gray said that two queens "facing each other" indicates gossip.

The whole notion that it mattered whether or not these cards faced each other was interesting. But then something happened that made a light go on.

The first deck I bought as a young reader, after working with the Waite-Smith, was called the Sacred Rose Tarot. It's a beautiful deck that I used happily for years, but after a personal tragedy, I stopped reading the cards entirely for a period of time. When I picked up tarot again, I felt I could no longer read with the Sacred Rose, the deck I'd been using when tragedy struck, so I went back to the Waite-Smith.

In addition to the remarkable art and vibrant colors in the Sacred Rose, one distinction of this deck is that almost every figure is in full portrait. Very few cards are in profile or even three-quarter face; the figures all face forward. When I switched decks, it was like an explosion of angles and connections. I remembered that line from Eden Gray, and I was blown away by how much I could now see. It was like the tarot doubled or tripled in potential meaning.

Any two cards in a layout, whether next to each other or not, have some kind of relationship with each other—some kind of interaction. They look at each other, or away from each other. They are back to back, or both facing the same thing (perhaps a third card), or they ignore each other (absence is as significant as presence, remember). Every pair of cards has some sort of connection. In a simple five-card layout, that's a total of ten different paired interactions, any or all of which can add meaning to your reading.

More so than almost anything else we learn about tarot, these interactions depend upon the individual deck being used, as my example of the Sacred Rose shows.

Death is one of the rare cards in the Sacred Rose that doesn't face forward; it looks to the left. Death in the Robin Wood Tarot looks straight ahead. Death in the Waite-Smith deck looks to the right. How Death interacts with other cards depends entirely upon which deck is used; the same layout with different decks will produce different results.

Reading Paired Cards: The Professor

Let's take another look at the Influences reading from chapter 4 (illustration 20). This was a reading for a professor with career issues. In this five-card reading, the three cards in the middle face straight ahead. The Star (on the right) looks to the left, and the King of Wands (on the left) looks to the right, so that these two cards seem to face each other.

Here I would say that the benefactor (King of Wands) is concerned about, and is paying attention to, the health and well-being (Star) of the querent. Since these two cards look at each other, we can perceive a connection. In the meantime, the other three cards, representing short-sightedness, injustice, and struggle, look straight ahead and do not interact with anything else in the reading. Since we know that absence is as important as presence, we can read this forward-looking posture. It's like these cards are *refusing* to interact. Each is saying, "Don't distract me!" *Don't distract me from my focus on money,* says the Four of Pentacles; *Don't distract me from my struggle to get through,* says the Chariot—perhaps feeling he won't get through if distracted; *Don't distract me from my decision by pointing out its unfairness,* says Justice in reverse, seemingly indicating that Justice cannot be influenced by a plea for sanity from the Star.

Here we could advise the querent to pay a little more attention to her benefactor, even if it's a distraction. We could also advise her not to bother trying to plead for justice, since it will fall on deaf ears. We could point out that the benefactor is the only person looking at the querent, including the querent, who is not, in any of the cards about her, looking directly at her health situation.

Now, as long as I'm using this particular deck (Robin Wood), Justice will *always* face forward. Does that mean pleas for justice are always to be read as useless? Not at all! Here's where pattern recognition comes into play: the cluster of forward-facing cards underlines this lack of interaction and makes it notable.

Imagine a grouping of cards facing Justice (reversed or upright). In this case, we'd perceive an interaction, even though Justice doesn't look back at any of the other cards.

Reading Paired Cards: The Dancer

Refer back to the Vitruvian Man reading in chapter 4 (illustration 29). In fact, bookmark this reading, as we'll refer back to it again. Here, I read the cards for a former dance student who had recently moved into his own apartment.

About the head cards (Strength and the Star reversed), I said: "Because Strength literally overlays the Star reversed, we have reason to suspect that the querent is trying to overlay underlying fears with outward behavior; he's trying to stuff the fears away by being loving and kind and so on."

Now we can add to that interpretation using our understanding of how a pair of cards can interact. Strength and the Star, in this configuration, are looking at each other and are nested together, almost like a yin and yang. This reinforces the earlier interpretation: Strength is looking at the Star and responding to her. We see she's looking compassionately at the inner darkness (Star reversed) and treating it with her characteristic compassion and kindness. Perhaps this means the querent is trying to be gentle with himself; his Strength is looking with kindness upon his dark feelings. In fact, the right-hand cards in this reading advise the querent to do exactly that: be gentle with himself, since the Eight of Swords in reverse is a card of fragility.

Whole Layout Interactions

When we look at pairs of cards interacting with one another, we're seeing them as part of the same picture or living tableau. In fact, we can see the entire layout as a single piece of art or a single scene. We can start by understanding that each individual card is the reproduction of a piece of art—a painting, drawing, collage, or photograph. You might think about "art" only when you consider something like the Dali Tarot, which was created by a world-famous artist, but it's not fame that makes someone an artist. Every card was created by an artist, whether Pamela Colman Smith, Robin Wood, Mary Hanson-Roberts, or any other illustrator. So when we're looking at a tarot card, we're looking at something that follows the principles of artistic creation, and understanding art can help us understand tarot.

Furthermore, a five-card layout isn't merely five pieces of art or ten interactive pairs; it's a whole, a single picture with five sections. It's easy to liken a tarot layout to a comic-book page because the division between panels strongly resembles the division between cards. On a comic page, each panel is whole—its own moment, thought, or action, with a breath or a pause in the "gutter" (the space between panels), followed by another moment, thought, or action.

But we can also liken a tarot layout to a work of fine art, and understand its flow by looking at art.

Illustration 33: Rendition of The Birth of Venus *by Sandro Botticelli*

Consider Botticelli's *Birth of Venus* (illustration 33). Most of us recall "Venus on the half-shell," the goddess rising from the sea on an enormous shell, clad only in her flowing red hair. The goddess is the central image.

But Venus is surrounded by three other figures in the painting, and part of what makes her image so central and primary is that the other figures look at and move toward her. Every line we see supports Venus as embraced, encompassed, supported, and focal. A figure to her left (our right) moves to clothe her, and the trees above that figure echo the line and angle of the cloth. The figure on our right looks up and at Venus, while the figures on our left look down and at her.

If we imagined for a moment that this painting were a three-card reading, it would be easy to see that the center card was supported left and right, and that the other two cards were aligned in purpose, looking toward each other and focused on the same thing.

With *Birth of Venus*, the grouping flows toward the center, but there are lots of other possibilities.

Illustration 34: Rendition of A Sunday Afternoon on the Island of La Grande Jatte *by Georges-Pierre Seurat*

In George-Pierre Seurat's famous *A Sunday Afternoon on the Island of La Grande Jatte* (sometimes known as *Sunday in the Park*, after the musical *Sunday in the Park with George*), we can immediately observe two things about the overall flow of movement (illustration 34). First, the painting is very still. People are at rest, relaxed. Second, almost every-one is facing to the left (toward the river Seine). Again, we could easily imagine a configuration of several cards in which most face to the left. In chapter 4, we learned that the left can be the side of the unconscious or the side of the past, depending upon the layout. So cards laid out so that they are all facing left could indicate a trend toward the past—but not, in the case of this painting, a rapid movement in that direction. It's all rather languid.

Whole Layout: The Dancer

Let's continue looking at the reading that I've named "The Dancer" (illustration 29), from chapter 4.

The Knight of Cups (in the left-hand position) looks to the right, while his horse angles up and right. This means he rides directly toward the head position, where Strength looks down and left, directly at him. I see these cards as connected, sharing a single message. In fact, the Her-mit reversed (also in the left-hand position) seems to be looking in that direction as well.

This reinforces the ideas I already had about this reading: that the choice between dark gloominess and being in the world in a loving way was a choice seen in both the head and left-hand positions. This will happen often—you'll see things throughout your reading that will continue to deliver the same message over and over. This is a sign you're doing well! Sure, there's more information to discern the more you look at the cards, but it's also true that if your message is accurate, you'd expect it to be consistent. It would be downright odd if a pat-tern in a layout contradicted an interaction between cards, for example. Everything in the layout is reading the same querent asking the same question, so there should be a motif you can discern. Readings will say move forward or look back; something good is coming or it isn't; speed up or slow down. By the time an "outcome" or a "what to do" card is dropped at the end of a reading, that card rarely comes as a surprise. (If it does, revisit the entire reading, looking for anything that points to it.)

I wondered previously if dance could be a key to the querent feeling better about himself. As I look at the layout, it seems more and more that other cards move toward the Page of Swords (in the right-hand position). The Knight of Cups seems headed his way, even as he's looking at Strength. The Sun seems to be making a beeline diagonally across the reading, suggesting that leaving the garden (in the card) is a physical activity that the Page can support. The Sun also shows an infant, while pages represent young people, further connecting these two cards.

I'm intrigued by the two foot pairings: the Sun/Seven of Wands reversed and the Six of Swords/Seven of Cups reversed. The first card of each pair shows a journey, and the second of each is a reversed seven—life's journey stalled by a lack of willpower. When you look at the angles and lines of these four cards together, they don't seem to go anywhere. The Sun moves diagonally toward the Page of Swords, but movement across the bottom of this layout is minimal. The Sevens appear to be blocking momentum and progress. With the Seven of Wands, the diagonal line of the wand in the hands of the warrior moves down, out of the bottom of the layout, into nothing. The Seven of Cups is a static card that seems to look nowhere. Even with two journey cards in this section of the layout, the overall impression is of things going nowhere. This gives us some insight into our problem cards, and is in strong contrast to the leaping movement in the "should do" area.

Illustration 35 shows the flow of movement in the Dancer reading. There's the small back-and-forth at the head position, a larger arrow at the same angle from the Knight of Cups to Strength, a straight line from the Knight of Cups to the Page of Swords, and a diagonal line from the Sun to the Page of Swords. The line across the bottom (from foot to foot) is straight, matching the straight line from hand to hand, but has no arrowheads, as the bottom seems static.

There is, you'll see, an aesthetic quality that makes these twelve cards a single picture. Look at the center cards, in the spirit position. The World has a round frame mimicked by the visible part of the Ten of Pentacles. There's a stillness to this center, as if it says *Here I am,* while all the motion swirls about it, almost as if the wisdom that Spirit has to offer the querent is just waiting for him to notice.

Let's continue exploring interactions among cards with a brand-new reading.

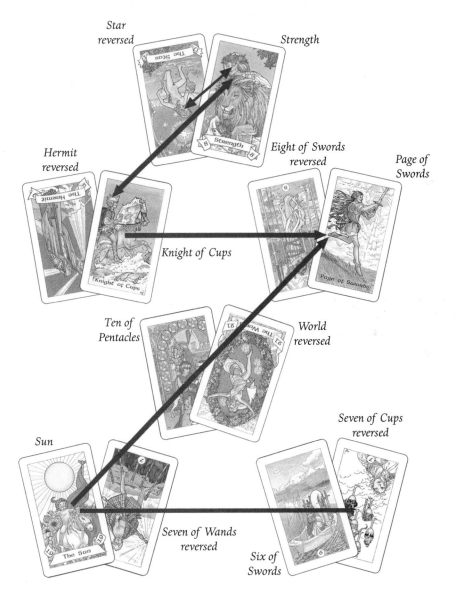

Illustration 35: Flow of Movement in the Dancer Reading (Robin Wood Tarot)

Whole Layout: House of Sorrows

The following reading brings up an interesting problem for a tarot reader: What happens when the cards seem to be addressing two different issues? What if there are two patterns that don't seem to intersect? Here, the flow of movement can help us discern the story being told.

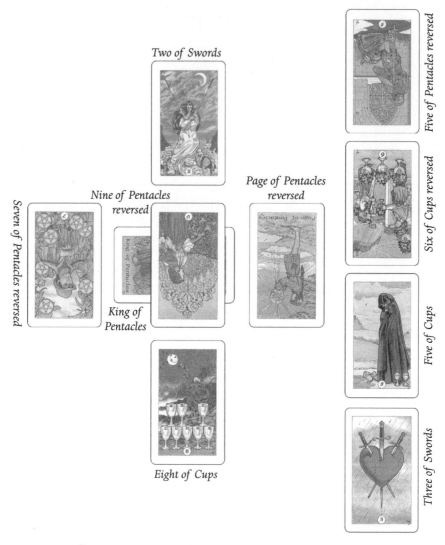

Illustration 36: House of Sorrows Reading (Robin Wood Tarot)

The pattern in the House of Sorrows reading is almost staggering: fully half the cards are pentacles! There are no majors at all, so we know the issue isn't life-altering in a larger or more spiritual sense, but there are two fives, so there are plenty of changes afoot. Of the remaining cards, three are cups, which is a notable number (see the Distribution of Cards chart at the beginning of chapter 3). There are no wands. Interestingly, when I was giving the reading to the querent, I determined that he wouldn't be able to build anything permanent, but I failed to note that, without wands, nothing can be built. I found the information from the other cards!

When the reading began, before any cards were laid out, the querent told me he was having a lot of problems with his house. Heavy snow had burdened a roof already in need of repair, and when the weather warmed and the snow melted, he ended up with a flood in his living room. Under the circumstances, I could only laugh when I turned the first card and saw the Nine of Pentacles reversed, which means minor disasters in the home, such as theft, intrusion, physical issues with the house, or other disruptions such as legal issues. It was easy to see that this card pertained to his current predicament.

As all the cards were laid out, finances took a large role, and with the pentacle pattern, that made sense. The King of Pentacles struck me as a money person withholding repair funds—I asked the querent if he'd been denied a home improvement loan and he said no, but he'd just met with the insurance adjuster and the news wasn't good. The Seven of Pentacles reversed suggested to me that there had been problems with the house for a while; that the querent's unhappiness with his living situation had been growing for some time, as the results of his hard work were no longer worth it. He acknowledged that he'd put a lot of effort into the roof already.

As we read the cards, the pentacle pattern kept us focused on the home, including the disappointing outcome: that any improvements would be temporary and anything fixed would need fixing again (the Five of Pentacles reversed means temporary shelter; based on home-repair issues being so prevalent in the other cards, this was an obvious interpretation). But another pattern emerged.

The cups in this reading are sorrowful; the Eight and the Five both express different kinds of dissatisfaction. The Eight of Cups has to do with the wisdom to know that one's material possessions are not what's important in life. *These "things,"* the Eight says, *don't satisfy me. I will walk away from them and seek something true to myself.* The Five of Cups is different, and it is unwise. *I am bereft. I've lost everything,* the Five says, weeping over the three spilled cups, never seeing the full cups behind him. With the Five of Cups, the normal interpretation is that the querent *hasn't* lost everything; he just thinks he has.

The two cards are different and yet similar. In the deck I'm using, they both depict a cloaked figure in relation to a group of cups on the ground, and they both have mountains of trouble in the background. (But note that the moon in the Eight of Cups provides light and wisdom, while the clouds in the Five prevent the querent from being able to see clearly.)

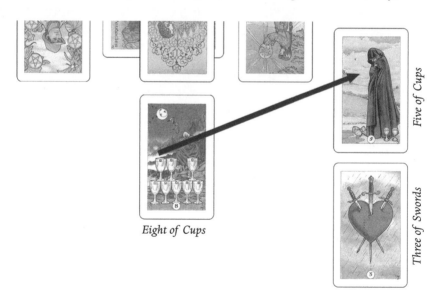

Eight of Cups

Five of Cups

Three of Swords

Illustration 37: Eight of Cups to the Five of Cups

There is also a visual relationship between the cards in this Celtic Cross layout. I showed the querent how the mountains in the foundation card seemed to be leading him to the mountains in the self-image position. Keeping his distance from the troubles of his home / situation /

cups was building into a deeper feeling, turning him into an unhappy person. Instead of the problem being a foundation, a thing, it was becoming how he saw himself. One card was on a path to the other, as shown in illustration 37.

Once we see this, it is natural to look at the third card in this reading that depicts a form of dissatisfaction: the Seven of Pentacles reversed. Its meaning is as different from the Eight and Five of Cups as those two are from each other.

The Seven of Pentacles is a card about the fruits of one's labor. The upright card shows satisfaction: the person has worked hard and sees the results. Reversed, the picture is the same: a person sees the results of his labor, but now he wonders if it was worth the trouble. The profit is just not commensurate with the effort required to earn it.

Upon examination, we see that the Seven of Pentacles in this reading is, like the Eight of Cups, also looking at the Five of Cups (illustration 38).

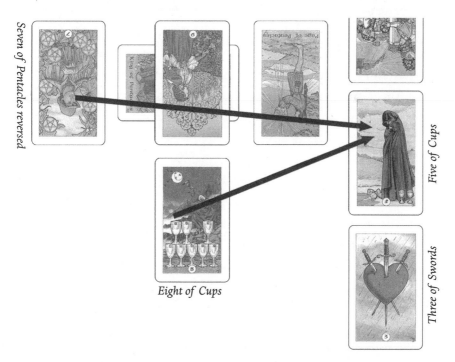

Seven of Pentacles reversed

Eight of Cups

Five of Cups

Three of Swords

Illustration 38: A Triangle of Dissatisfaction

Now a story has begun to emerge. The querent is a person with good values, who is able to distance himself appropriately from problems and not take them too seriously. He can walk away when need be. This may mean "emotional distance" in both positive and negative ways, but clearly, with all the house troubles the querent has, it has been helpful (Eight of Cups). In the recent past, though, he's begun to see that the amount of effort he keeps putting into this house is just not worth it (Seven of Pentacles reversed). Somehow, this frustration has become incorporated into how the querent feels about himself. Instead of being a person with some financial and household struggles, his nature has become doleful. How did this happen?

The key to the sorrowful cards in this reading was the tragedy of the Three of Swords.

The Three of Swords is a card of terrible heartbreak, and here it appears in the environment position. The querent has recently had an awful tragedy in his family. The line from the Three of Swords that drew my eye was the straight line of the central sword. The tragedy was shooting up, through his self-perception, through his hopes and fears, straight into his outcome (illustration 39).

The querent was beginning to perceive his house troubles as deeply painful, because the tragedy was coloring his perceptions. He was losing perspective because of the influence of this line of pain running up through all ideas and feelings about the situation. It is as if all the inconvenience and struggle was, itself, becoming tragic and awful. But all of this is the influence of the Three of Swords.

The lines of movement show us how these two separate patterns interact (the pentacle/money/house pattern and the cups/sorrow/tragedy pattern). On the surface, they seem to be two separate issues. Only when we look at the movement do we see the cards touching one another.

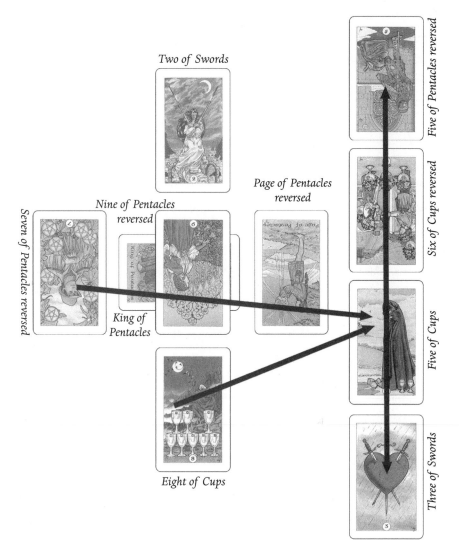

Illustration 39: Movement of the Three of Swords

Cards Determining Other Cards

Cards interact with each other in many ways. We've just explored how they can look at each other, away from each other, or mutually toward a third card. There's much more.

Sometimes a sequence or pattern can lead you to a card interaction, just as visual information can. After all, when you lay out a reading, you're seeing the entirety of it at once: cards, layout, patterns, sequences, and visual flow are all laid out before you. The idea isn't to go through a checklist of interactions in your head, but to see the reading as an organic whole, a living intercommunication.

Consider court cards. Often confusing to readers, the meaning of a court card can frequently be determined by its interactions with other cards. A pattern of court cards, we've learned, is a social situation; lots of court cards means lots of people around.

In the House of Sorrows reading (illustration 36), we find two court cards. This is exactly average for a ten-card reading, so we can't call it a pattern. Yet the fact that both cards are pentacles, one in the crossing position and one in the ahead position, suggests that they might interact with each other. They aren't looking at each other particularly, but they seem connected.

In this reading, I told the querent to expect more bad news, similar to what he'd heard from the insurance adjuster. "More of the same," I told him. The Page of Pentacles here looks like the child of the King of Pentacles, or a repetition of the King. My instinct was to completely throw away a standard interpretation of the Page of Pentacles and see the card interaction as an echo—after all, there aren't two Kings of Pentacles in the deck, so if the situation is going to recur, or something similar is going to happen (a different assessment by a different person with the same sort of outcome), a second card must serve to indicate that.

I read an *echo* when two cards seem to be serving identical purposes; they are near each other, but are not actually looking at each other.

Another way you might see an echo or repetition is when two cards are so similar that they seem to underline the inevitability or importance of a concept.

If one card is an *outcome* of another (separate, that is, from an "outcome" position in a layout), there will be something in the position of the cards or the lines in the art to indicate the directionality—one card must look like it comes from the other.

If one card is an *avoidance* of another, the two cards will look away from each other, often in a back-to-back position. This could be denial in a psychological sense, or an attempt by the querent to get away from an unwanted situation.

One card might be a *reflection* of another. This is similar to an echo, but it's the same sort of situation showing up in multiple parts of a querent's life—ripples in a pool. Ripples are all outcomes of a stone being thrown or a frog jumping or something like that—they share a common cause. When two cards appear to be reflections, a third card is apparent as the cause.

An Echo, a Change of Direction

This example shows a rather remarkable echo, and it also addresses ways in which a reader can make a mistake and still course-correct to the benefit of the querent.

My querent was a regular client, someone I have worked with every few months for several years. Our most frequent subject for readings has been her career. I knew the reading was about a decision, so I used a Vitruvian Man layout. Illustration 40 shows the left-hand ("what I'm doing") position.

Illustration 40: The Six of Wands, The Sun (Robin Wood Tarot)

The Six of Wands is a card that often shows up in regard to career questions, as it indicates acknowledgment of success, rewards, and praise, as well as a potential journey. The Sun, read by itself, can also indicate a successful journey, although in this case, it is an adventure into the unknown. The child / Sun leaves the flower garden and ventures into the wide world. The bright sunlight follows him, indicating hope and blessings.

We might read these two cards together as emphasizing the inevitability of a positive journey into new opportunity, since the meaning of the two cards overlaps on these points. But here is where a visual reading is vital.

These two cards, in the Robin Wood deck that I used for the reading, simply *look alike*. Both depict a figure on a white horse, carrying a banner. They move in similar directions: the Six of Wands to the right, the Sun forward and to the right. The banner and tabard of the Six of Wands depict the Sun, while the red of the Sun's banner is the color of the Six's leggings. The rays emanating from the wand the Six carries are like the rays of the Sun, and occupy the same part of the sky. It is clear that the Six of Wands was designed to echo the appearance of the Sun card, although Robin Wood doesn't say so in her book, leaving readers to discover this for themselves. (You will find many such secrets embedded in well-designed tarot decks.)

The Sun, in the reading, overlays the Six of Wands, giving it predominance. In addition, the minor arcana card rather naturally is "less than" the major. The Six literally wears the Sun; he is reflecting the Sun's glory so that we can see his movement toward the Sun (he moves right and the Sun card is to his right) as indicating that he is fundamentally *about* the Sun. So instead of just reading the "meanings" of the cards, we know that the journey, the success, the praise, is taking the querent toward the Sun—the echo, here, indicates a larger meaning.

But here's the twist. At this point, the querent interrupted me to say that this time, the reading wasn't about her career. She was concerned about having children and fertility (another very common question that every professional reader hears regularly). A doctor had suggested that she was probably not fertile and shouldn't try to conceive.

This happens from time to time in a reading: sometimes there's a disconnect between the querent, the cards, and the reader. Once, I was the querent who received such a reading. I asked for a reading because my relationship was in flux, but the cards made no sense when applied to my relationship. Suddenly I realized that the cards made perfect sense when applied to my writing! In fact, I attribute my first book to that reading. The cards answered a question I wasn't asking. Here, instead of refocusing the querent, I refocused the interpretation.

Illustration 41: The Full Reading (Robin Wood Tarot)

My first view of this reading was that it was career-oriented. The Six of Wands and Eight of Pentacles both suggested this, and I began to talk to the querent about her career. There was nothing wrong with what I was reading; in fact, the querent confirmed that the career information was accurate—it was just not what she was asking about. The first, career-based reading was still accurate, but was not important to the querent at that moment.

There are no cards here (illustration 41) that are obvious fertility indicators. (In a reading, the Empress or the Queen of Pentacles might promise pregnancy in the near future, and the Star might be a health-related blessing.) The Queen of Swords reversed can indicate infertility, but that card is in the head position in this spread, indicating that's what's on the querent's mind.

On closer examination, though, I found a pattern. Children are the dominant image in three of the twelve cards: the Sun, the Page of Cups, and the Eight of Pentacles. (Children are also visible in the background of the Six of Wands.)

The other pattern is sixes—there are two—so we know the querent is on a journey. At first that's not helpful; it's like, of course she is! But then we look at the Six of Wands again and can ask ourselves, *Is she journeying toward a child? Toward the Sun-child?*

More and more, the Sun-child is looking like a central card. The Page of Cups seems to be looking at it, as though the glowing idea that emerges from the Page's cup *is* the Sun (illustration 42).

My tarot teacher always called the Nine of Cups the "wish card." Upright, you get your wish; reversed, you do not. Here, the card is in the position of the right hand ("what you should do") and is paired with the Eight of Pentacles. The Eight is another card often associated with career; it is the student who is improving his craft. Once focused on the question of fertility, I saw that the wish was paired with another child.

The Vitruvian Man layout doesn't have an outcome card; instead, the right-hand position is what the querent should do. *Go for it,* I told her. *If your wish is for a child, pursue that and ignore any naysayers.* Her doctor makes an appearance in this reading; he is the Knight of Swords, whose news causes upheaval. He is paired with the Chariot reversed and is moving swiftly toward Temperance reversed. It's clear his news has upset the querent's inner balance (Temperance) and self-control (Chariot).

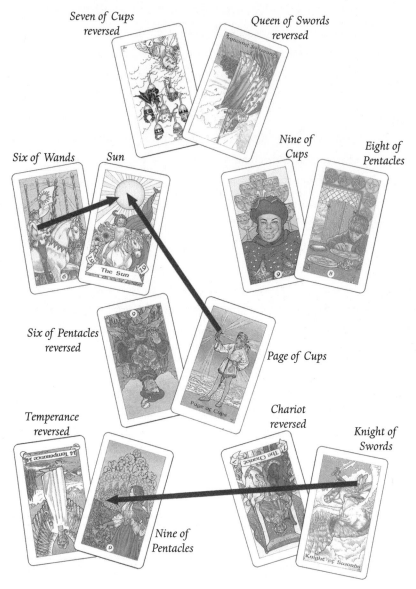

Illustration 42: Movement in the Infertility Reading

In this reading, an echo opened my eyes to the direction and flow of the reading, and the querent redirected my idea of the subject matter. The cards continued to tell the truth through the change of subject.

Homework: Studying Movement in Art

Homework Questions

Look up the following fine art paintings (they're all famous and easily found on the Internet), and see if you can determine the flow of movement in each.

1. *Guernica* by Pablo Picasso

2. *The Girl with a Wine Glass* by Johannes Vermeer

3. *The Dancing Class* by Edgar Degas

4. *The Creation of Adam* by Michelangelo (from the ceiling of the Sistine Chapel)

Homework Answers

These answers are my own perceptions. If you see something different, that's fine.

1. The overall flow is from right to left, with several figures looking up. The upward-facing figures appear to be looking for a heavenly response, but they are actually gazing at a light bulb. The sense of movement is rapid and chaotic.

2. In this painting, the three figures are looking in three different directions. The girl looks away from the gentleman (a suitor?) and toward us, while the gentleman is focused entirely on her. Based on posture and flow of movement, it seems he is interested in her and she is not interested in him, even though she smiles. The figure in the background is disinterested, looking away from them both. His stillness is mirrored by the stillness of the painting on the wall. The mood is somber, and movement is slow and stately.

3. The student in front of the mirror is the focal point. The grouping to the left is paying attention to her, and the musician appears to be playing for her. The three students behind and to her right are definitely not paying attention to her, looking purposely

away or lost in their own practice. The overall flow, though, is around the central figure, just as in the *Birth of Venus*.

4. In this depiction of Creation, neither God nor Adam is central; rather, the empty space where they meet is the focal point (hence the many reproductions of just that central space: their hands). The landscape on which Adam rests serves to further divide the entire space into Adam's side and God's side. They look toward each other, with the angels mostly mirroring God's movement toward Adam.

Exercise: Reading Card Interactions

In this exercise, I'm going to walk you through a real reading that I did for a paying client (for this reading, and all others in the book, I obtained permission from the querent to photograph and write about the readings). We'll return to this reading in the next chapter, to see what stories it tells.

If you have the Robin Wood Tarot deck, you might find a better sense of connection by laying out the actual cards before you, rather than working with illustration 43. Although some specific details of the reading are illuminated by Robin Wood's artwork, you could also lay out the Waite-Smith or a similar deck, while referring back to the illustration.

1. As always, take a few deep, cleansing breaths before you begin.

2. The querent said: "I am recently divorced, and I am wondering about my love life."

3. Start reading the cards, writing down or recording your interpretations. Then answer the following questions, and read my thoughts and the querent's.

Illustration 43: The Lonely Love Life Reading (Robin Wood Tarot)

Questions

- What patterns do you see?
- What do you think the patterns mean to the querent?
- What interactions exist in pairs in the same position (head, hands, etc.)?

My Thoughts

In this twelve-card Vitruvian Man reading (see illustration 28), I see the following patterns: There are two threes and two aces. There are five wands and zero cups. All of these are unusual.

The querent is asking about love, but there are no cups. However, we know that the question is about love. There's a *desire* for love, so shouldn't there be cups at least in her head? I interpreted the suit patterns to mean that the querent's desire for love was not for romance (cups) but for someone with whom to build a life—because wands are about building things.

Threes are outcomes, and both threes are in the head position: she's wondering what will become of her. This reinforces the interpretation I have for the wands: she both wants to know her outcome (what will become of her) and wants to know about the life she will build. These are related concepts.

The left-hand position shows a card of rebirth (Judgment) and a card walking away from rebirth (Ten of Wands). It's as if it's saying, "Okay, I'm reborn. Now where am I going?" I interpret Judgment to mean that the querent's divorce was positive for her; she's reborn, but the interaction in that position seems to say that she can't stay with a positive interpretation. The Ten of Wands walks away from Judgment: her burden is too great to enjoy the powerful change in her life.

The left foot is the position of where she's recently been. There's an ace there, so there was a recent new beginning. It overlays and covers a reversed Queen of Wands. Because of the wands pattern and because of the position, I decided the Queen was the querent; these are her wands, so this is her. The Ace of Wands in this particular deck is exceptionally phallic. The beginning seemed therefore to be sexual (a new man) but negative (the Queen is reversed). Perhaps it began and ended? The life-affirming qualities of the Ace seem to cover the negativity of the reversed Queen, so I suggested that she'd had an affair that ended badly but was in some ways validating: She felt sexy and desirable, and her doubts about "Can anyone want me?" were erased.

In the right-foot position (where she's going), the interaction is between two major arcana. There isn't a major (or minor) pattern in this reading, but two majors in the same position suggest that her next decision could be life-altering.

The Querent's Response

The querent agreed that she wanted to build a life, and the burden of the Ten of Wands was the thought of building that life alone.

Discussing the Ace of Wands/Queen of Wands reversed, she acknowledged that she'd recently had a brief affair with a man that had ended badly. It was indeed exciting and sexy, but she was feeling wounded.

Questions

- Looking at the whole reading, what is the general flow of movement?
- Where is the Five of Swords reversed looking?
- How can the negative Five of Swords reversed, in the position of "what Spirit/God wants of you," be interpreted in light of where it is looking?
- What do you think is the relationship between the Queen of Wands reversed and the King of Wands reversed?
- What do you think is the relationship between the Ace of Wands and the King of Wands reversed?
- What other interactions do you see among cards across the layout?

My Thoughts

I see a general flow toward the right side of the reading, toward the future. Six (half) of the cards appear to be moving "off stage" toward the right. Three look straight ahead, with only three cards looking elsewhere. I understand the querent to be moving into her future. I don't think she's dwelling too much in the past, and if she is, she needs to be discouraged from doing so.

The Five of Swords reversed appears to be looking at the Six of Pentacles. This is interesting, as there is a cheat or deception, possibly a theft (the Five), which is looking at a generous gift (the Six). Could it be that something stolen will be returned? Does that make the King of Wands reversed the thief? There is no particular movement interaction with the Ace of Pentacles, but it is the beginning of a financial venture. Perhaps the theft is related to this new venture. I asked the querent if she'd loaned her ex-lover money.

There's obviously a connection between the King and Queen of Wands. If her face wasn't covered by the Ace of Wands, they'd be looking right into each other's eyes. If the Queen and the Ace of Wands represent an affair, then perhaps the King is her ex-lover. Ex-lover and thief? The connections seem to be telling an unhappy story.

The Ace of Wands isn't pointing at the King. Instead, it appears to be pointing at the Three of Wands reversed, who is, in turn, looking at the King of Wands reversed. The Three of Wands reversed is waiting and waiting for something that will never arrive. It appears that the querent wants her ex-lover back. The Ace, which is the beginning of their affair (and his phallus) moves toward waiting (the Three), which looks toward the King (her ex). The reversed Three suggests she's waiting in vain.

The most difficult part of this layout is the center, the position of "what Spirit/God wants you to do." We've already seen how this position seems to be telling a story about the querent's recent past: the investment in her lover and his betrayal. How can that represent a higher purpose?

Looking again at the way the Five of Swords reversed looks at the Six of Pentacles, we see that he seems to be looking at a response to being deceived. Spirit, here, is showing us that the deception can look at a generous and kind card, a card of charity and goodness. The Ace of Pentacles, representing a financial beginning that was tainted by deception (the Five of Swords reversed), can also represent a new beginning within oneself. I think the message of Spirit here is to forgive the deception and begin again. Forgiveness is a message that makes sense in this position, and we can interpret the Ace as a beginning in response to the deception, a renewal that connects the card to Judgment in the upper left. Thinking about the connection, and looking again at Judgment and the Ace of Pentacles, it's easy to see the visual similarities: both round and golden, both forward-facing. The Phoenix rising in Judgment seems star-shaped with her arms outstretched (just as the Vitruvian Man himself does). I can suddenly perceive that she is shaped like an Ace of Pentacles, and this reinforces the message that this particular ace represents renewal.

The Querent's Response

The querent had loaned her ex-lover money, which she never expects to see again. As we spoke, it became clear that she misses him and wonders if she will ever have him back, and she even misses her ex-husband. This surprised me, as I saw Judgment in such a positive light; I underestimated the power that the Ten of Wands had. Otherwise, she found what I had to say accurate.

We will continue this reading in chapter 6, so hold on to your notes and questions!

SIX

Interaction with Language

Throughout previous chapters, I've had cause to say things like "this tells a story" or "this forms a narrative." Tarot interacts with language in that it creates and is created by language. In other words, tarot readings form words: phrases, sentences, and stories. And words, and the structure of language, can help form a tarot reading.

The Grammar of Tarot

Why should studying grammar matter now? Either you studied it in grade school, or you didn't and you've gotten along just fine without it. But the grammar of tarot can help you deepen your readings. The words and phrases that constitute a reading should make sense and should have life. Too many people find that tarot readings just sit there, flat and lifeless, like a list of facts.

Consider the readings we've already explored.

In chapter 4, we talked about constructing a narrative from a Past-Present-Future layout. Instead of saying *this is the past* and *this is the present*, it's important to weave them into a story. The guiding principle I offered was: [past] *and therefore* [present], or [past], *but now* [present]. In grammatical terms, past and present are treated as *independent clauses*, with a conjunction or a conjunction phrase connecting them.

An independent clause is a whole idea, complete unto itself. Each clause could be a whole sentence, but the connecting phrase forms a more complex sentence from the two clauses together. Does that sound like gobbledygook? Let's go straight to the cards.

In chapter 4, we used the following interpretation of the past card of the Ten of Swords and the present card of the Nine of Wands: *In the past, you were defeated, and therefore, you are now guarded, cautious, and distrustful.*

"In the past, you were defeated" is what I mean by an independent clause. You could use it as a whole sentence. It has a subject ("you") and a predicate with a verb ("were defeated"). "You are now guarded, cautious, and distrustful" could also function as a whole sentence. The subject again is "you," the verb is "are," and there is a dandy string of adjectives.

The long sentence connecting past and present is lively; it could be the beginning of a screenplay if "you" was replaced by "our hero." Instead of just rattling off the qualities of each card, forming phrases and sentences into a story allows you to make the reading truly animated.

Tarot Words and Sentences

Sometimes a card isn't going to be a whole sentence (or clause). Perhaps it's just a word or phrase. And here it can be very helpful to remember parts of speech.

When you first learn to read tarot, there is a tendency to read every card as a noun or an adjective. The Ten of Swords is "defeat," and the Nine of Wands is "cautious, guarded." Indeed, most of the simpler guidebooks will give meanings in just this way.

Instead, try looking at an entire reading as if it's a sentence. In this way, you'll see that a reading needs nouns and verbs, adjectives and adverbs.

Nouns, you may recall from grade school, are *persons, places, or things.* This means they're specific and individual, and when a reading seems particularly vague, it might help you to look for the nouns. Often, a noun is what is known about a reading, and a noun is a commitment, by the reader, to a definite focus in the reading. (Remember, in chapter 1 we learned that such commitment helps the Psychic Child to come out.) When you say something like "the Emperor is *your boss*" or "the Two of Cups in reverse is *your former job*," you are using nouns to make your reading grounded and specific.

Verbs are *action* words. "Doing" and "being" are actions, and finding the verbs in a tarot reading helps the reader understand behavior. "Happen" is also a verb, and querents obviously want to know what is happening. A reading needs to address some or all of these questions: What is the querent doing now? What has he done in the past? What will he do next? What should he do? What should he avoid doing? Verbs are an important part of the majority of the questions that a querent has, yet when you learn the meanings of tarot cards, verbs are largely absent!

Adjectives describe nouns (your job is *difficult*), and adverbs describe verbs (things are happening *quickly*). Your reading will give information about nouns (the specific Who-What-Where that every journalist is taught to ask) and verbs (what is happening, will happen, might happen, happened in the past, etc.) and should also be descriptive. The Knight of Swords is not just a man but an aggressive man; without the adjective "aggressive," there's no real information.

Sample Grammatical Reading: A New Job

The querent asked me, almost tongue-in-cheek, "Will my awesome new job be awesome?" I used the six-card Yes/No layout from chapter 4 (illustration 44).

The first thing that struck me about the reading was the strength of the no. This isn't just no, it's *no way!* The only upright card is the one that depicts the querent leaving the "awesome" job.

The next thing I saw was the twos. Fully half of these cards are twos, and there are twos in literally every position: a two each in the past, present, and future. *Everything* is about balance, I saw, and everything is out of balance.

Finally, there are four cups—two-thirds of the reading. The querent cares about feelings, even while talking about her job.

What is the grammar of this reading?

Page of Cups reversed   *Two of Swords reversed*   *Two of Pentacles reversed*

Two of Cups reversed   *Four of Cups reversed*   *Eight of Cups*

Illustration 44: Yes/No: Will My New Job Be Awesome? (Robin Wood Tarot)

To answer that question, the task here is to find nouns, verbs, and descriptive words in each time period—past, present, and future—and to find how they connect. Connections are almost always conjunctions, remember, and are usually *and therefore* or *but now*.

I'd been asked specifically about a new job, one the querent had accepted but hadn't yet started. It's easy, then, to assume that the cards of the past have something to do with the old job or the reason she left it.

Here's what I said: *You felt unsupported in your old job. Your relationships there had broken down, and you were unstimulated. You weren't learning anything or being inspired in any way.*

The noun for the Two of Cups reversed is "relationship," and the adjectives are "unsupportive" and "broken/damaged." The Page of Cups reversed is a person (noun) whom I identify as the querent. The adjectives are "unstimulated" and "uninspired"—no ideas emerge from the Page's cup of inspiration and wisdom.

So far, we have no clear verbs. We don't know yet what's happened. So we look at the present: *You got tired of waiting. You were frustrated by being in limbo, so you made a move without knowing all the facts. You just assumed that the things you couldn't see were okay.*

I relied rather heavily on my Psychic Child here, but I think you can see exactly where this information came from.

The Two of Swords reversed is the end of a period of waiting, and there's a suggestion of unwise action. Perhaps the person in this card is still blindfolded and acting without fully completing the waiting period. The upright Two of Swords is someone who doesn't know all the facts, isn't ready to make a move, or is stagnating in a difficult or dangerous situation. The basic situation isn't necessarily reversed when the card is reversed; there is still danger, but the person is now acting, moving. Here, then, is our verb.

The Four of Cups depicts someone who hates what he has, without realizing there is something even better available. In reverse, this card is someone who embraces the possible, who sees that he can act and can embrace the blessings life offers.

Together, the present cards show someone who has embraced a course of action, even when it wasn't quite time. Seeing the blindfold, and noticing the way that these two cards seem to align, I think that the Four, too, isn't seeing everything there is to see.

The querent jumped into a new job because she was tired of waiting for the right opportunity. She probably accepted the first job offer she got, and she didn't ask a lot of questions during the interview process.

Our verbs, then, are "acting," "accepting (the job)," "ignoring (the facts)," and "assuming (that it would all work out)." We know what happened: the querent jumped on a job offer with little information. Our verbs are specific and descriptive.

Now we can look at the future: *You're not going to be able to keep your balance at the new job. You're going to be stressed and overwhelmed. You're going to hate it, and before too long, you're going to walk away. The only good part is that, when you do go, you will have really learned important lessons and will have grown from the experience.*

The meaning of the Two of Pentacles reversed is being overwhelmed, out of balance, and stressed. It's all adjectives. Here I added a noun: the new job. It was easy, in this case, to figure out the noun since the querent told me her question! I've also got a verb, and again, it was easy to guess that a card showing a person walking away was an action card. The Eight of Cups is a card of progress (as are all eights), and here it is about leaving something behind even though it's still good (since she's going to hate her job, I'm guessing "good" means prestigious or lucrative) for a higher level of some kind. This I interpret as lessons learned. With five reversals in this reading, I'm going to look at the one upright card as very positive, and look to it to help the querent. Here, it tells her to leave.

The querent was quite satisfied with this reading. She confirmed the accuracy of my description of her past job and of how she accepted the new one. She was willing to suffer in this new job for a while to build her resumé, and she interpreted the Eight of Cups as exactly that— she'll be able to walk away with better credentials in her field, and the awful stress will have been worth it. This was interesting for me, because, like many readers, I always find it awkward (or worse) to give bad news to the querent. Here I had a querent who was excited about the future, and I told her the job would be a terrible experience. But instead of taking it badly, she took the news in the best possible light. It was a lesson for me in being a truthful reader and facing the darkness squarely.

Obviously, when reading the cards, I didn't just use grammar. Indeed, you can see that I used all the techniques we've learned so far: interaction with pattern, interaction with layout, and cards interacting with each other, as well as trusting my Psychic Child. Language is one more component, one more interaction, that adds depth to a reading.

Most importantly, I think that looking at the grammar of a reading helps you avoid common mistakes. Grammar helps to prevent you from simply reciting meanings, or even meanings-in-position, and allows you instead to turn the reading into a narrative. This narrative can be applied to the other interactions we've learned. For example, the pattern can be telling a story; it can be a noun, verb, or adjective. In fact, the layout itself can determine the grammar. Consider our Vitruvian Man layout, with positions for "doing" and "should do." If you're interested in designing your own layouts, having room for a range of storytelling words is an important component to consider.[7]

The Tarot Subject

Here's another thing that I remember from grade school: a teacher writing a sentence and asking us all to figure out what was the subject and what was the predicate. The subject is the noun that the sentence is actually about, and the predicate is, well, everything else. In the sentence "My boss is a jerk," the subject is my boss. In the sentence "I hate my job because my boss is a jerk," however, *I* am the subject; it's about how I feel. The boss is just part of the description of why I feel the way I do.

These are exactly the kind of sentences that might show up in a tarot reading. In the previous example, "My work is unsupportive" and "I am uninspired" were two sentences (based on the Two of Cups reversed and the Page of Cups reversed, respectively). "Therefore, I hate

---

7. With this in mind, perhaps you could revisit the exercise that closes chapter 4.

my job" is implied, especially because the cups pattern indicates strong feelings.

Now, there are some interesting things going on with these sample sentences about the jerky boss. First, "because" is a conjunction, a connecting word, so you might see "I hate my job" as one card, "My boss is a jerk" as a second card, and "because" as the space between them.

As examples, a Seven or Eight of Pentacles reversed or a Ten of Wands might indicate unhappiness at work, while the Emperor reversed or the King of Pentacles reversed could be a jerky boss. Any of those cards might also mean other things, but pairing them might cause you to derive this particular compound sentence.

The other thing to notice is that in the sentence "My boss is a jerk," the subject is not the querent.

One of my pet peeves regarding the tarot is what I call the "psychotherapy syndrome." Every tarot reading is treated as a psychotherapy session, and every card is treated like a component of the querent's psyche. Nothing is ever about other people or other things. This is why the environment position is so important in the Celtic Cross layout, and why the Influences reading is so helpful. These layout positions point *away* from the querent, to other people, places, and things (nouns). You want, as a reader, to be able to see past the inside of a querent's head and heart and into his whole world. Not only does this make for a better reading for the querent, but the challenge is greater for you, and gives the Psychic Child greater opportunity to step forward.

This is not to say that the psychological aspect of a reading is without value. Far from it! Discovering the querent's inner feelings, her secrets, her dreams, is very much a part of a tarot reading. Just as the Celtic Cross has an environment position, it also has one for hopes and fears. Indeed, that position is inherently psychological, as it implies that one's hopes and fears are one and the same! In chapter 4, during the sample Influences reading, I suggested to the querent that a card represented the subconscious, while the querent insisted it was another person. Contrary to avoiding the psychotherapy syndrome, I was insisting the querent was the subject while she thought the subject was a particular dean.

The trick is not to eliminate psychology, but to incorporate it along with an understanding of the outside world. Let the querent be the subject, but let other people, places, and things be the subject as well, depending upon the card. Have an open mind to the language of the tarot, and interact with it intuitively, letting the Psychic Child guide you.

Sample Reading: Another Person's Reading

A friend contacted me with a request for a favor. He'd done a reading for himself and was having trouble interpreting it. Could I look at the reading and help?

This is a situation I've found myself in quite a few times, where someone else asks for my aid with a reading. It's tricky for a number of reasons. First, it's simply not my reading. As discussed in chapter 1, a reader develops unique, personal interpretations for various cards over a period of time. Many people don't treat the Four of Wands as a card of marriage, but I do. Contrarily, Waite sees the Five of Cups as a troubled marriage, but I never use that meaning unless other nearby relationship cards demand it. So for someone else to lay out a reading, with their own understanding of card meanings, and then ask for my opinion, of necessity means that my take will be different, not because the other person is wrong, but because we each have a take on the cards that is uniquely our own.

Another problem here is that the other person may be using a deck I don't know well. If it's the Waite-Smith, or Hanson-Roberts, or Robin Wood, or some other deck I use myself, then it's not an issue. In the sample reading I'm about to discuss, the reader/querent used the Deviant Art, which is a deck I've never used. I don't connect with that deck, so I chose to read largely based on the cards as I always understand them, not based on the Deviant Art illustrations—so right away a piece of my ability to flow with the reading was lost.

The final barrier is the lack of psychic connection—to my cards and to the experience of the reading. I haven't touched or laid out these cards; I'm just looking at them.

Despite all these issues, I do find I can give effective input in these situations, and I have always said yes.

My friend sent me a simple reading of a unique layout. (Since the layout was invented by a mutual friend, I chose not to "steal" it for this book.) It was a layout of the snapshot type, giving facts and advice about a specific situation—in this case, my friend's romance.

The last position in the layout was explained to me as "What am I not seeing?" The King of Swords was here.

The cards and our conversation revealed that my friend and his boyfriend had recently broken up, that he felt it was temporary, and that he was waiting it out. A twos pattern emphasized the couple-ness and the waiting. I asked him to send me a picture of the reading so I could look at it and see lines and movement.

Immediately I saw the Two of Cups to the right of the King of Swords. In the Deviant Art deck, the King of Swords looks to the left, so he was looking away from the Two. I asked, *Is it possible he cheated on you?*

Here's the Two of Cups, one of the most romantic cards in the deck (the card I used on my own wedding invitations), and here's another man, disconnected from it, looking away from it. *Another man.* In addition, the other man was looking to the *left*, making me feel that the ex was cheating with someone from the past.

Absolutely not, my friend insisted. He suggested that the position "What am I not seeing?" could be a secret (cheating) but could also be something like "What am I in denial about?" or "What do I know but refuse to acknowledge?" In truth, that could still be cheating, but I had given my friend the information and then proceeded to give him a different interpretation. *It's possible*, I suggested, *that the King represents qualities that your ex has.* The King of Swords is judgmental, sharp, perhaps arbitrary, perhaps cold. I suggested that he might not be seeing that this situation could recur, again and again, and not just be a one-off. *If you get back together,* I said, *there might always be times when he is like this, when he pushes you away. This won't be the only time you go through something this harsh with him.*

Fundamentally, my friend and I disagreed about what or whom the *subject* was for the statement represented by the King of Swords. I believed the subject of the secret was the ex: he is keeping a secret. My friend thought he, the querent, was the subject: What am *I* not seeing?

Was the King external—a situation in the real world—or internal—something my friend was thinking or feeling? Although my friend and I disagreed, it was, ultimately, his reading, so I offered an alternate interpretation and left it at that.

About three weeks later, it turned out there was, indeed, another man from the past, although he might not have been in the picture at the time we did the reading.

Subject/Object

What's important here is the question of subject. Instead of thinking of sentence structure, you might think of subject/object. The subject is the one with a point of view, the actor. The object is acted upon. When feminists talk about women being "objectified," it means they are being treated as if their role is to be acted upon: gazed at, pursued, desired. All of which is great *if* you also get to be the subject: gazing, desiring, and having a point of view all your own. In a relationship, two people are both subject and both object; they love and are loved, they each have views and desires, and each is desired and viewed.

In the sample reading from the last section, we struggled to determine if the querent was the subject of secrecy (keeping what he knew from himself) or the object (someone else was keeping a secret from him).

There are a number of cards in a standard tarot deck that have inherent subject/object questions. The Seven of Swords is an example.

The Waite-Smith deck (and Robin Wood after it) depicts a thief. The meaning is theft or betrayal. But is the querent the subject or object of theft? Did the querent steal, or was the querent robbed?

Psychotherapy syndrome has the querent as the subject of almost everything, as if there's no outside world with which to contend. It's powerful, then, to look at a reading as if it contains *different* subjects and objects, as if the querent is engaged in the world and the world engages back. Interacting with the language of tarot helps that happen.

Storytelling

Another way to interact with language in a tarot reading is through storytelling: turning the entire reading into a narrative tale.

This is a book about interacting with the tarot, and not about story structure or narrative arcs or any of that, but we can briefly look at the elements of a story and how they can become a part of your tarot interactions.

The *protagonist* is always the querent. While the querent may be the subject or object of a specific tarot card, sentence, or phrase, the reading as a whole is ultimately a story about the querent.

There is a *goal* or incentive. In a story, it can be anything from "save the world" to "boy meets girl." Often, the querent's question relates to the goal. It might not be expressed that way, of course, but the querent has something in mind, whether it's a relationship, a new job, or something else. Maybe the querent isn't aware of any such goal and simply wants life to go well, day by day. That, too, is a goal.

There are *obstacles*. Maybe it's a villain—a rival or an authority figure causing trouble—or maybe it's the querent's own bad behavior, or perhaps it's fate. If the querent's question isn't about the goal, it's about obstacles that are getting in her way. In Greek tragedy, the hero has a fatal flaw that causes his own downfall, often by ignoring the will of the gods. This is tremendously interesting for the tarot reader, who can help a querent see his own shortcomings and also show him what is inevitable or inescapable (usually connected to the major arcana) so that the querent can accept his fate and avoid the pain and tragedy of fighting it.

In addition, there is often, in a story, a guide or some kind of *help*. In the hero's journey, the mentor is a key figure in the tale. For purposes of tarot, we can look to the reading to see what people or conditions help the querent.

Of course there is a *resolution*. Whether happy ever after or tragic, there is an outcome to facing the obstacles: They are or are not overcome. The lovers end up together or they don't. The ship sinks or it doesn't. With tarot, we can help the querent see the outcome of the steps she is currently taking, so that she can decide if she likes that outcome or not. If not, we can go back to the story and see what plot points have to change in order for the end result to change.

In a story, the protagonist also has some sort of *character arc*. Generally, we expect the hero to grow, change, or progress in some way (unless he's James Bond: 007 never changes). Look to a reading to see the opportunity for growth that the goal and obstacles present.

We can look at sample readings already presented in these pages and see if they fit the basic story structure.

The Influences sample reading in chapter 4 (illustration 20) has a simple narrative. The querent's goal is to do well in her career. The obstacle is the way the institution conspires against her ever getting tenure. Help comes from the dean who is represented by the King of Wands. The pattern of major arcana suggests there aren't a lot of options for her except to keep doing what she's doing (fate plays a role). Thus, the character arc is limited—she doesn't seem to grow much here. The outcome is that she continues to struggle and continues to succeed, but just barely.

What about the sample grammatical reading at the beginning of this chapter, "A New Job" (see illustration 44)? The querent's goal is two-pronged: to advance her career and to enjoy her new job. She will achieve one goal (career advancement) at the expense of the other. The arc—the potential personal growth—is enormous, and the obstacles are considerable. Here is a situation that will cause immense suffering but will ultimately be rewarding. It's an opportunity not just for the querent to advance her career, but for her to learn about herself, and about walking into situations unprepared. She will have no allies in this and will have to rely on herself.

Just looking briefly at these two readings, we can see how storytelling can add another whole layer to the interaction with a reading, and how it is also a powerful interactive tool with the querent. Telling querents a story engages them and lets them see their own journey.

Homework: Sentence Structure

I asked the question "How is my day going to go?" and laid out the following three cards (illustration 45):

Queen of Swords   Page of Wands reversed   Nine of Pentacles
reversed

Illustration 45: Three-Card Day Spread (Robin Wood Tarot)

Homework Questions

1. What is the subject in the question?

2. What is the object?

3. Which card or cards represent the subject?

4. Which card or cards represent the object?

5. Which card or cards represent a verb?

6. Which card or cards are adjectives about the subject?

7. Will my day go well or badly?

8. What parts of speech (nouns, verbs, adjectives, adverbs, conjunctions) might be represented by the Queen of Wands? By the Page of Wands reversed? By the Nine of Pentacles reversed?

9. Form a sentence based on these three cards.

Homework Answers

1. The subject is "my day."

2. I am the object; "my day" will have an effect on me.

3. I think "my day" is the Nine of Pentacles reversed, although you might have drawn a different conclusion.

4. The Queen of Wands clearly seems to represent me, since I asked a question about my day and I am a woman, who would typically be represented in the tarot by a queen. By the way, it was a very sunny day when I laid out these cards, so the sunshine seems to reinforce that that's me during this day.

5. If I am the first card, and the third card is my day, then the second card, the Page of Wands reversed, is the verb that acts upon my day.

6. I am going to go back to the third card. This card is not just "my day," but a description of (adjective about) my day.

7. Simply reading patterns will tell you that two reversals in a three-card reading isn't good.

8. The Queen of Wands is the object/noun (me) as well as adjectives about me.

The Page of Wands reversed is a verb (acting upon me or my day) and may also be a noun (a person who acts) and adjectives or adverbs (describing the person or the actions).

The Nine of Pentacles reversed is the subject and a noun (my day) as well as adjectives describing my day.

9. There are many possible sentences. Here's mine: *I will approach the day happily but will be thwarted by someone else's mood or negative message, and will end up frustrated at home.*

The sentence can be broken down as follows:

Queen of Wands: Me, approaching my day with bright sunshine. The noun "me" is modified by the adjectives "happy" and "sunny."

Page of Wands Reversed: The verb is "thwart." My day is thwarted by a moody (adjective) person (noun) or a negative (adjective) message (noun).

Nine of Pentacles Reversed: My day (noun) ends with me frustrated (adjective) because (conjunction) I'm stuck at home or something happens at home that isn't good.

You'll notice that every card had adjectives associated with it. This is because tarot cards are vivid and descriptive.

If your interpretation was different from mine, that's okay.

Homework: Subject/Object

Page of Pentacles   Seven of Swords

Illustration 46: Two-Card Homework (Robin Wood Tarot)

Homework Questions

1. For the reading in illustration 46, form a sentence in which the Page of Pentacles is the subject and the Seven of Swords is the object.

2. Now reverse it: the Page is the object and the Seven is the subject.

3. Can they both be objects?

4. Can they both be subjects?

Homework Answers

1. *The querent is a student who gave generously to an unworthy person who didn't repay him.* The querent/subject gave generously, and the thief/object is the unworthy recipient of generosity.

2. *Someone (perhaps the querent) has been stealing or sneaking off with money or gifts from someone younger and more naive.* The thief/subject stole from the Page/object. Be very careful when you think the querent is the subject in a case like this. A querent is likely to become offended if accused of stealing! It may be necessary to tell

a querent he is a thief, but it's usually best to ease into it, as I did in this sentence by saying "perhaps the querent."

3. For both cards to be objects, a third card should be the subject. If the querent was robbed (object of the Seven of Swords) and also has received generous help from a young scholar (object of the Page of Pentacles), then a third card would generally indicate who the querent is. There's no sentence structure otherwise.

4. Yes. The querent can be both the student and the thief. Look to other cards to determine who was robbed, if you can.

Exercises

Exercise: Sentence Structure

This exercise will guide you through the analysis of a simple reading, such as the previous homework reading, using sentence structure.

1. Before you begin, formulate a simple question. Now look at the sentence and determine what the subject is.

2. When you're ready to begin, take several deep, cleansing breaths, and center yourself.

3. Ask your question out loud.

4. Shuffle the cards until you feel it's time to stop.

5. Lay out three cards, from left to right.

6. Do you see the subject of your reading? Which card is it? The subject is a noun. What adjectives describe this noun?

7. Do you see the verb in your reading? Which card is it? The verb acts upon the subject or object. What adverbs describe the verb?

8. What other parts of speech do you see?

9. Form a sentence about your reading.

10. Repeat this exercise several times, until you feel confident in your ability to read sentence structure.

Exercise: Subject/Object

This exercise will also guide you through the analysis of a simple reading, such as the previous homework reading, using sentence structure.

1. Begin by taking several deep, cleansing breaths, and center yourself.

2. Shuffle the cards until you feel it's time to stop.

3. Lay out two cards, from left to right.

4. Read the cards out loud as if the first card is the subject and the second is the object.

5. Now reverse it: the first card is the object and the second is the subject.

6. Can you form a full sentence for each version of the reading?

7. Repeat this exercise several times, until you feel confident in your ability to read sentence structure.

Exercise: Lonely Love Life Revisited

In this exercise, we will continue the Lonely Love Life reading from chapter 5 (illustration 43), this time looking for story and narrative.

Again, you may do better setting up the reading with your own cards to look at, to allow yourself to really feel the reading. Take some breaths to center yourself before you begin.

Questions

1. The Vitruvian Man layout (illustration 28) gives the querent a choice: Where you're going (right foot) versus what you should be doing (right hand).

   • Tell the story of what happens in the case of the right foot.

   • Tell the story of what happens in the case of the right hand. Remember, the right hand is the position of "what you should be doing" and should be the preferred choice (if they are different).

- Is it a different story if you tell it about all four cards? What's that story?
- Remember that these stories are about a reading we've already begun. The story should make sense for the protagonist who has already emerged in this reading.

2. What is the querent's narrative arc? In other words, what is the protagonist's journey?

3. What are the goals, obstacles, and resolution?

4. Are there any allies?

5. Is there wisdom to be gained?

6. Write your thoughts in your journal before reading my response.

My Thoughts

Before telling the story of the right hand or the right foot, I recall that there are other stories in the spread.

The story of the left hand is, *The querent has been reborn, but she is so overwhelmed that she cannot enjoy her transformation. All she sees is the burden she carries.* The left hand has a beginning and a middle, but no resolution.

The story of the left foot is, *The querent wasn't feeling too good about herself, but an affair awakened her sexually, and then hurt her.*

Now we can get to the right foot. Two majors in this position indicates she's entering into an important period, and her next decisions are crucial. The Magician denotes a person (often a man) of considerable personal ability. He's the "whole package." The altar before him has the four tools of the tarot, indicating he has equal power over all aspects of life. In general, I wouldn't think that the Magician is misusing his power unless he's reversed, but Strength reversed gives me pause.

Strength is a card that represents a clear choice between the power of compassion (upright) and the power of brute force (reversed). It is often a spiritual card, and a card that reveals deep psychological states of being. With this card combined with the Magician, in a reading that is oriented around relationships, and keeping in mind that the querent has already made a bad choice about a man, I read the story of the right foot as: *You will meet a man who seems to have everything and be everything you want. You'll be attracted to him for his strength and ability, but he is not a good-hearted or kind man. He may be a man from the past or someone you (the querent) don't know yet.* This last part was in response to the querent's question "Is it my ex-lover?" Maybe. The cards don't say.

Once again, this is a story without an ending. That's where the right hand comes in. I could not have understood the right foot without seeing the right hand as its counterpoint.

In the right hand, we see the King of Wands reversed. Read on his own, he is often an older (over thirty) man with a difficult temperament. He tends to be bossy and abrupt. But he is paired with the Six of Pentacles. This is a card of generosity; it can mean the querent receives a gift or help of some kind—there is a benefactor. This card often means a person (the benefactor), although it can also be read as a situation.

The story (or chapter) of the right hand, "what you should be doing," is this: *The querent will meet someone who is awkward and perhaps even unpleasant. As she gets to know him, though, she'll find that he is generous, charitable, and good.*

Combining the right hand and foot, I get the following: *The querent will end up in a position of choosing between two men. One is obviously attractive and seems to be the one she wants, but she should instead look at the other one, the one she initially didn't like. If she pays attention to this man, she'll find him to be truly good, someone who will give money instead of taking it, someone worthy of her.*

Looking at this choice, and at the Six of Pentacles, I asked the querent if she was involved in any charity or community service work, and she said no. I suggested that she might get a call in the near future, asking for her help in some community, church, or charitable project, and that she should say yes. It seems like, with the Six where he is, and the story told in that position, she might easily meet this particular man while doing such charity work. It also seems consonant with what Spirit wants for her—to look away from the past and forgive, charitably.

Previously, I interpreted the King of Wands reversed as the ex-lover, and now I'm saying the Magician is the ex and the King is someone new. How can this be? The interactions of movement told a different story than the interactions with layout and with language. This is fine. There are many stories within a single reading, which is how so much information can be gleaned from only twelve cards. The beauty of reading interactions is that they're *not* all the same. By reading the movement interaction and the interaction of the meaning of the card in the position of the layout as two separate things, I can find more stories to share with the querent, more sources by which we may uncover truths together.

The querent's narrative arc is as follows: She had a transformation (the divorce), which began her journey. She faced multiple obstacles, first in feeling burdened and alone, and then in being betrayed by a lover (plot twist!). Her goal is to find the right man, or to be happier and less burdened by her own aloneness (although she *really* doesn't like that option). Her ally has yet to be met—he is the benefactor seen in the Six of Pentacles. Perhaps he is her future lover, or perhaps he'll help her find him. Her true wisdom will come not when she finds a lover, but when she lets go of the past and learns to forgive.

THE QUERENT'S RESPONSE

The querent listened attentively to all I had to say and promised to make another appointment soon. As of this writing, I do not know the end of the story.

In my years of reading tarot, I've developed a grudging acceptance of not necessarily knowing how stories turn out. It can be frustrating, but as long as I know I've helped in the moment, I can live with it.

SEVEN

Interaction
with the Querent

If you've been observant, you've seen that we have been discussing interactions with querents throughout the previous six chapters. The energy of the querent is imbued in the reading just as the energy of the reader is. This isn't all metaphysical mumbo-jumbo; in addition to the more occult meaning of energy, which is certainly present, the querent has concerns and questions, as well as a personality and style of communication. All of this will affect your reading. There are lots of ways in which a querent can actually make your reading harder. This may seem counterintuitive: Why would someone ask for a reading, perhaps pay for a reading, and then impede the reading? We'll look at the answer to that question shortly. There are also ways in which a querent can make a reading easier, although we, as readers, have to beware of allowing ourselves to rely on them.

Types of Querents

As I see it, there are four types of querents, and each brings his or her own challenges to a reading:

1. Yourself

2. Friends and family

3. A paying customer who is a regular client: someone for whom you read weekly, or monthly, or irregularly on an ongoing basis

4. A stranger; often someone you will never see again after the reading, such as a customer at a psychic fair

Establishing a Connection

Whoever the querent is, it's important to establish a connection to him or her. I like to feel that there are three "people" in the reading—me, the querent, and the cards—and we're all connected.

Susan, my first teacher, taught me to shuffle the cards, then hand them to the querent to shuffle. First I have the querent pick a significator, handing him four appropriate court cards (having decided whether my querent is a page, knight, queen, or king—if I'm not sure, I can ask). I say, "Choose the one you feel is you." That word "feel" is important, because I don't want what the querent *thinks, believes,* or has *decided.* I want the querent to be in an intuitive state. I then shuffle until I feel the deck is clear of any prior readings, then hand the deck to the querent, instructing him to visualize his question flowing into the cards. "Don't concentrate," I'll say. "Just see the images like a movie montage." Experience has taught me that many people are intimidated by meditation and are convinced that they can't concentrate or aren't good at concentrating, so instructing querents to visualize can make them stiffen up. While the querent shuffles, I focus on the significator, visualizing the querent's face on the card.

Next, I ask the querent to cut the cards into three piles, from him to me, then I pick them up in such a way as to reverse the order of the three piles (illustration 47). I make sure we both use our left hands, since left, in the occult, is the side of the unconscious. The hand-off of cards at the cut helps us connect, too.

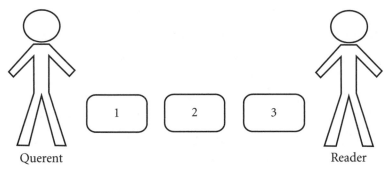

Illustration 47: Three Cuts, from Querent to Reader

All of this is great for long consultations and establishes a deep rapport. However, at some point I started doing things like parties and psychic fairs, where I had to work quickly, one reading after another, bam, bam, bam. All that shuffling and cutting and so on took too much time for a fifteen-minute reading.

I learned that making eye contact, handing the cards back and forth just for the cut, and taking a few deep, cleansing breaths could replace having the querent shuffle, and even the significator was unnecessary. (It's still nice to have a significator, especially when working for a phone or Skype client, but in a rapid-fire situation, I've learned to do without.)

I should point out, though, that I was reading for three or four years before I felt comfortable dropping these extra steps. In addition to establishing a connection, these steps help anchor and ground the reading, and they help the Psychic Child to come out. If you drop them and find there's a loss of clarity in your readings, trust your feelings and add them back.

Always let the querent touch the cards if the reading is in person, and work out a substitute if the reading is over the phone or Skype. (My phone readings go like this: *I'm going to run my thumbnail up the side of the deck. Tell me when to cut. Okay, I'm starting now.* The querent tells me to cut, and we do it again twice more.) At one psychic fair for charity, the organizers were rushing the readers because a long line had formed. Instead of having the querent cut the cards, I just had each person hold the cards for a moment. That brief touch was enough, under the rushed circumstances, to create the connection.

Reading for Yourself

The querent can be the reader—you can read for yourself. Some people read *only* for themselves, and some *never* read for themselves. For me, if I just want to look into this or that, I'll read my own cards—it's a good way to just check in or to get short-term information, and it keeps me on my toes. On the other hand, if something serious is happening, I'll get someone else to read for me.

In learning to know your own Psychic Child, it helps to know what your blocks are. For me, when I care very, very much about the outcome, I get a little "head-blind." Once I did a reading that predicted disastrous results, blew it off as a mistake, and then was blindsided when the disaster happened. The reading was both right and wrong—the information was correct, but I didn't take it seriously. Ever since, I've reached out for support in situations where really listening to the reading is crucial.

If you read for yourself, I highly recommend reading out loud. Vocalizing does things to the psyche that make a huge impact on a reading. Spoken language uses different parts of the brain than does merely thinking to yourself; more neural connections are made, and this helps to open the deeper mind. You may have noticed this yourself. Have you ever thought through a problem and been stuck, and then gone to talk it out with a friend? Often, you'll discover the answer just by verbalizing the problem, before your friend has even spoken. This is the power that the spoken word opens up in the brain: you send the thoughts to the brain's speech center, and along the journey, synapses fire. It can be an awakening.

When reading for myself, I will pretend that someone else is in the room, and read to that imaginary querent, or even have someone close to me sit in the position of the querent and read to that person.

Reading for Friends and Family

When you first pick up the tarot, you will be reading only for people you know: yourself and those close to you. This can present some serious challenges that you should be aware of.

You usually know the issues going on in the lives of the people you love. You know their relationships, their jobs, and the things that bother them. It can be easy to zoom in on what you know in the querent's life and immediately apply this information to the reading, without opening yourself up to psychic knowledge.

When I was young and had been using the tarot for perhaps a year or two, I did a reading for one of my sisters. (Given that it was over twenty years ago, I no longer remember every specific card, but I do remember a lot of the content.) At that time, this sister was involved with a theater group in which there was a lot of gossip and back-stabbing. She had wormed herself into that group and was a relative newcomer, and she was very concerned with holding her position and being accepted.

The reading suggested dishonesty, theft, and a terrible outcome. I recall a Page of Swords reversed and a Seven of Swords, and perhaps also a Five of Pentacles reversed. I told her she'd be the subject of gossip and dishonesty, that some kind of theft would be involved, and that she'd end up being ousted from the theater group. We talked a lot about that group, those people, and how the entire situation might play out.

A few weeks or months later, we discussed the reading. By that time, she was well established in the theater group, and key people had accepted her as a friend. The gossip that had plagued her when she first joined was no longer directed at her, and she felt comfortable in her role. She brought up the reading: What could that have been about? How could it have been so completely wrong?

At the time, she was working in retail. Looking back on when I did the reading, we realized that she had been fired from a job shortly after. A coworker had stolen from my sister's register; my sister was the one who came up short, and the thief successfully made it look like my sister was to blame. Point by point, everything that I said would happen had, in fact, happened, but in a different situation, with a different group of people.

This was one of the most important lessons I have ever learned about what happens when you dampen the presence of the Psychic Child, and I always keep it in mind. If you, based on your mundane, day-to-day knowledge, declare right off the bat what the meaning of the reading is, then you don't allow the cards to tell you, and you don't allow the Psychic Child to step forward. Your own preconceptions drive away the more accurate knowledge. In my sister's case, the reading was correct, the cards were correct, and my Psychic Child guided me to an accurate narrative about what would happen. But because I was sure I knew the whys and wherefores, I didn't listen to my inner voice. Listen? I didn't even *ask,* so there was no opportunity to listen for an answer.

There are times when you think you know the answer, just as I thought I knew in the case of my sister's theater group. In chapter 5, the House of Sorrows reading (illustration 36) was for a friend, and as I saw the first card, I was sure it was about the situation with his house. Right away, I said, "This looks like it's about your house," and explained the meaning of the card. Laying down the crossing card, I again explained the meaning, and suggested it meant a person controlling money. I asked him if he'd met with such a person. By suggesting, instead of stating, the part of his life this related to, and by asking questions, I slowed myself down enough to make sure I didn't ride roughshod over a hidden meaning; that the obvious didn't overwhelm the subtle. This interaction allowed us to fine-tune the reading. I was right about the subject matter: the Nine of Pentacles reversed was about his house. I suggested the King of Pentacles might be a loan officer; the querent corrected me—it was an insurance adjuster.

Another potential issue with friends and family is that it can be inhibiting. The better you know someone, the harder it can be to tell the person difficult news or to reveal something potentially embarrassing. It's important, when doing a reading, to have some privacy. People will sometimes say, "Oh, it's fine if s/he stays in the room and hears this." If this person has never had a reading from you before, though, she may not realize that a reading can reveal something deeply hidden.

When I was in my early twenties, I had a boyfriend who was quite taken with my ability with tarot and told his family all about it. So much so that, when he invited me to his family's Christmas gathering, he asked me to bring my cards and do a few readings. Wanting to impress my boyfriend's family, I agreed.

Fortunately, I insisted on a private room, because I sat down with a cousin, laid down the first three cards of a Celtic Cross, and turned beet red. As I recall, the cards were the Lovers, crossed by the Queen of Cups, with Justice in the near future position. "You're having an affair and planning on leaving your wife," I blurted out. I was correct. Needless to say, the whole thing was extremely awkward and made me intensely aware of the dangers of reading for family. The querent was an in-law in the family; it was my boyfriend's cousin he was cheating on. I never saw that particular person again, but I learned my lesson. Be careful who is around when you're reading, be cautious when agreeing to read for family, and tell the truth, because it'll come out anyway.

Regular Clients

Paying clients bring up, for many people, personal issues around money. What is it okay to charge for a reading? How do I ask? How do I set a price? These are difficult issues for many of us, and whole books have been and will continue to be written on the subject.

It's okay not to charge. You can choose to be an amateur reader forever. I think it's a mistake in life, and a peculiarly American one, to assume that everything you do well is something that must bring income.

There are some advantages to charging that have nothing to do with having extra money in your pocket. One is, it forces you to become a better reader. Exchanging money puts a little pressure on you; you feel obligated to give the customer bang for his buck. While few people are foolish enough to charge for something they're not yet good at, there's no doubt you'll see improvement the minute you start charging. Money grounds the reading and makes it seem real. This impresses the daylights out of the Psychic Child, who will feel trusted and valued and step up to the plate as a result.

Charging for a reading also forces the querent to pay better attention. A friend or relative might think this is some amusing little thing you do. You might even feel that way when reading for yourself. But someone who has handed you money has handed you a different kind of trust and given the reading gravitas. This helps you do your work.

When I first began charging, I assured every client at the beginning of the reading that they could have their money back if they felt the reading wasn't worth it. That assurance was a way of giving myself permission to charge money without feeling like a jerk. There were one or two times, over the years, that I made good on that assurance. The reading went dead, I didn't feel anything, the querent felt nothing, and a refund was in order. Once or twice, that is, over dozens, perhaps hundreds, of readings.

I don't tell people that now, because I have much more confidence. I believe that the reading *will* work and there will be no need for a refund. I see no reason to say something that plants a seed of doubt. Of course, I would absolutely still provide a refund if it was the right thing to do.

How Much to Charge

My late ex-husband, Isaac Bonewits, used to say, "Charge your age." That was a good rule of thumb, but inflation finally outstripped it. Prices are also regional. You should certainly ask around, even going to a psychic fair and finding out what readers there charge.

As a beginner, give a discount for your inexperience. If the going rate in your area is fifty dollars, then forty dollars is probably appropriate for your first year. The opposite is also true, and given my experience level, I sometimes charge more than the going rate.

Regular clients, over time, will take on some of the problems of reading for family and friends: you'll get used to their issues.

In chapter 5, the infertility reading (illustration 41) was for a regular paying client. I am accustomed to reading primarily about her career. This client and a couple of others ask me career-based questions on an ongoing basis, which is quite interesting since most people are first and foremost concerned with love and family. I began the reading seeing job-type cards (the Six of Wands) and at once gave her information about her work. The querent redirected me to the fertility question.

As I stated in chapter 5, the Six of Wands and the Sun would have suggested career anyway, but the fact that I was pretty much expecting this client to ask about her career was a trap for me. I was fortunate that this client has a deep appreciation for how the psychic arts work (she is an astrologer) and so was comfortable asking me to change direction.

An advantage of reading for anyone regularly, whether yourself, those close to you, or clients, is that people have recurrent cards. This is a disadvantage to a beginning reader. If you are new, you want to get used to reading all seventy-eight cards, and reading the same people over and over will mean you see only a subset, as the same people have the same issues recurring in their lives.

What I mean, though, is a little deeper than just "Jane has a troubled marriage, so every time I read for her there will be complicated relationship cards," or "Joe has chronic health problems, so I should expect to see health-related cards every time I read for him."

Everyone has life issues specific to his or her own psychology, karma, and personality. For someone who regularly receives tarot readings, certain cards will come to symbolize certain issues. For one regular querent of mine, immaturity was an ongoing issue. This querent had Peter Pan syndrome well into adulthood, so we would look at pages and how they appeared in the reading. Pages symbolize young people and children. Often we'd find pages in this querent's self-image position when using a Celtic Cross layout. Once we established that it might not be great for a twenty-something or thirty-something person to see herself as a kid, we kept an eye out for those pages. Once you've had a few readings over a length of time with a page in the self-image position, it changes and colors the meaning of a page suddenly appearing in the crossing or the recent past position. Like a recurring dream, part of the meaning is in the recurrence itself, and this is a powerful force in your interaction with your regular clientele.

Reading for Strangers

The final category of querent is the stranger. I love reading for strangers. It is exhausting but exhilarating. There's a disinhibition that accompanies such readings. It's the "seatmate on the plane" syndrome: it's often much easier to bare your soul to a stranger than to someone you know, someone who will see you again and remember what they heard. Reading for a stranger is the opposite of reading for family and friends: there is no fear of revealing something if you know there will be no repercussions.

The circumstances under which one generally reads for strangers— at parties, psychic fairs, fundraising events, Renaissance fairs, and the like—are a downside for many readers, although that's a matter of individual taste. Such events can be intense, and chaotic, and demanding, and they can also be dull. At a fair, you might sit at a table, trying to "look psychic," waiting in vain for a customer to appear. It's more common, though, for a line to form, and it can be difficult even getting a sip of water between readings.

It's easy to complain about such circumstances, but many readers have noticed that the pressure cooker of doing one reading after another with little or no break increases their psychic abilities. The readings become more and more accurate, with more and more detailed information being revealed.

It is also my experience that strangers come to you with very serious problems indeed. I have done readings at fairs for such diverse individuals as a person with a persistent headache that may or may not have been a brain tumor, battered spouses looking for a way out, a drug dealer trying to get out of the business, a suicidal student at an Ivy League college, and a woman whose military husband didn't know she was pregnant. It's not enough, in such situations, merely to be psychic; you have to know how to do counseling as well, at least at the nonprofessional level, and it wouldn't hurt to have some emergency resources with you (like suicide hotline numbers and contact information for domestic violence shelters).

One downside of reading for strangers is that you don't get any follow-up. I've often thought of the woman with a persistent headache. That was a reading at a fundraising event. There were some dark, disturbing indications in the reading. The Star reversed and the Nine of Swords appeared; there was a nine pattern and she'd had the headache for nine weeks. She'd made doctor appointments and not shown up. I felt sure that this was a tumor or something equally dangerous. Without saying something inappropriate (*never* predict death to a querent), I urged her to see a doctor and said the omens were "serious." I will never know if I was correct, or if she saw a doctor, or what happened next.

Ask Questions!

Asking questions during a reading is valuable. Sometimes people don't want to do this because they think it means they're not really psychic (if you were psychic, the logic goes, you'd just *know*). Both readers and querents might think that asking questions is a no-no, especially if a querent distrusts occult things in general. But asking questions is actually a way to be psychic.

This looks like XYZ situation; does that sound right to you? By saying it this way, you can reassure the querent that, yes, you're seeing specific things and you're not on a fishing expedition. You can also assure your Psychic Child that you're listening to her voice (it's the Psychic Child, after all, who helps determine what "this looks like" when you say "this looks like XYZ"). The querent is asked only to fine-tune or redirect the reading.

This also goes back to establishing a connection with the querent. Even if all you did was make eye contact and hold hands for ten seconds, your querent is more likely to trust you: he feels connected to you and to the cards. When a connection is established, you, your Psychic Child, and the querent are all assured that the question is rooted in the context of the relationship, the interaction, and is not a con job that makes the querent do all the work.

As you become more and more talented as a tarot reader, you'll ask fewer questions because you'll be able to derive so much data from your interaction with the cards. But your querent will always be a part of your tarot interaction.

When Not to Ask Questions

As a beginning reader, you may ask a lot of questions rooted in insecurity. A lot of them may be "that can't be true" questions. For example, you see cards indicating an affair and think, "That can't be true," and then ask gently leading questions about the querent's marriage. This could be a successful strategy: the querent could reveal the affair, allowing you to go back to the cards and show why you asked the question in the first place. But these questions can undermine the Psychic Child's sense of safety as well as the querent's trust in you. When you interact confidently with the querent, you allow him to trust your abilities. This is particularly true when a querent is uncertain whether cards and tarot are legitimate at all.

Now, this may seem to contradict earlier advice. I've said to ask questions, and I've said not to make assumptions. How can you do that and avoid seeming unsure, all at the same time?

In truth, it's a balancing act. Give enough information, with specifics, to help both you and the querent feel that you've said something real, something grounded in real-world events and people, and ask questions based only on that information.

"Fishing expeditions" are something that people are warned against by those who are sure that all psychics are fake. "Fishing" is making vague, universal statements followed by leading questions designed to make the querent do all the work, such as "You were once unhappy. What's that about?" *Everyone* was once unhappy—you haven't really *read* anything, and anything the querent tells you at that point isn't really coming from the cards. This is very different from saying something like, "Your childhood unhappiness is affecting your ability to manage a project right now. I'm not sure what this childhood issue is about. Would you like to tell me?" In the following sample reading, I ask a question very much like that. The reason it's different is twofold: first, because I talked about specifics, relating a past unhappiness to a present-day project and management problems, and second, because I invited the querent to tell me (or not).

It's natural to find a lot of details in some areas and yet be confused or disconnected to other areas of a reading. Provide what details you can first, before asking questions, both because this allows the Psychic Child to come out, perhaps giving more details than you knew you had, and because it will build the querent's confidence. Then be honest about "this section here is a little unclear to me; let's see what we can figure out." This is very different from "fishing."

When I sit down to do readings, querents often ask if they have to tell me their question. I assure them it's entirely their decision. A querent who feels that the reading is based only on information she provided is not likely to trust the reading, and therefore is not likely to take the steps the reading, and the reader, says she should take.

Sample Reading: A Crucial Question

Another kind of question is when you see a situation but you can't place it in context. "What does *this* have to do with *that?*" is a legitimate interaction. You've been specific about one section of the reading, and about another section of the reading, and are not yet seeing how to put them together.

As I so often do when giving a reading, I started this particular one by asking, "Is this a yes/no question, a decision, or do you just want to know what's going on?" This lets me choose my layout.

"I have a decision to make about a health issue," she said.

I chose an Influences layout (illustration 48). Although normally I would have chosen the Vitruvian Man layout, which has a clear and obvious "what you should do" position, I felt like shaking things up and breaking my own routine. (This is something I do for my Psychic Child, to keep myself fresh and connected to the reading: I change decks and spreads whenever I feel a little stale.)

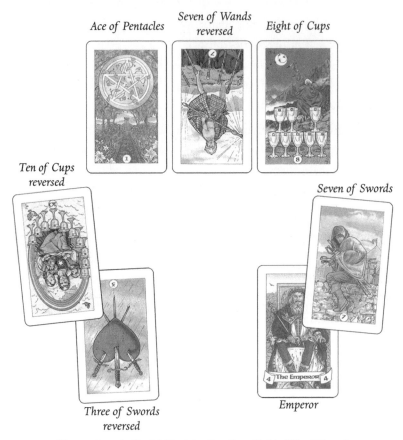

Ace of Pentacles

*Seven of Wands
reversed*

Eight of Cups

*Ten of Cups
reversed*

Seven of Swords

*Three of Swords
reversed*

Emperor

Illustration 48: Health Decision Reading (Robin Wood Tarot)

There are two sevens, so willpower and decision-making are crucial here. Right away we can see how difficult this decision is for the querent: the Seven of Swords is a weak card, a card of sneaking away and theft, while the stronger Seven (of Wands) is reversed. Otherwise, the reading is well balanced: two swords, two cups, one pentacle, one wand, and one major. No pattern there.

Since there is only one major arcana, this isn't a matter of life or death. That's a relief with a health reading.

Looking at the three central cards, I tell the querent that she's feeling off-balance and tired of fighting (Seven of Wands reversed); she just wants to walk away and not have to worry about it (Eight of Cups). The medical decision will cost money, and she's concerned about paying for it (Ace of Pentacles), but that's not a major concern. It's a new expense (aces are beginnings), but since the Ace is upright, I feel like she can handle it or is insured. Primarily, I see the stress of having to make a decision when she'd rather not.

The Emperor is a decision-maker. He's a leader or an authority, and as an influence, he's placed side by side with the thief: the Seven of Swords. The querent feels that someone else is taking this decision away from her. I suggest she's reluctant to cede to the authority of her doctor, who probably has already made up his mind.

The big thing, though, is the pair of influencing cards to the left. (In fact, during the reading, I addressed them first, and am only switching the order of the reading for purposes of writing it up.)

The Ten of Cups reversed suggests family issues. Its upright meaning is a happy family, fulfilled on a deep level that transcends simple wish fulfillment (which is the Nine of Cups) and addresses what truly matters. Reversed, it can be family fights, dysfunction (especially between parents and children), and loss. The Three of Swords is a card of tremendous grief and heartbreak. Reversed, it indicates that a grief has ended and wounds have healed, but scars are still present.

It's clear that something happened in the querent's family that caused her great grief, which she has healed from. That there was grief and subsequent healing means this is something in the querent's past, something she's had time to recover from. Somehow, this past sorrow is an influence on the current decision.

The querent and I interacted a bit about each section of the layout. She talked about her symptoms and her doctor and so on. I said there had been grief in the family and she agreed, but as we talked, I didn't see how this grief was connected. So I asked: *Somehow, this past grief is affecting your ability to decide about the medical procedure, and I don't understand that. What is it in the past that this current situation is bringing up for you?*

The querent revealed that some years back, her mother had a potentially fatal illness. The symptoms were not the same, but the querent's symptoms, though different, were consistent with the same illness. Her mother survived and is alive today, but might easily have died. The doctor was not concerned until he learned of the mother's medical history, and then decided to treat the querent's symptoms more seriously.

Suddenly it all connected for me. *You don't want to deal with these symptoms because doing so reminds you of the terrible pain of almost losing your mother. You were so overwhelmed at the thought that she might die that you've suppressed the whole incident, and now it's come back.*

It was an intense moment. Tears came to the querent's eyes; she could only nod. We hugged, and there was tremendous release. I was able to say that these symptoms had nothing to do with her mother's illness. I also said that it seemed as if she wasn't even worried about the diagnosis; it was facing the tests and making the decision that was causing her pain. Once she decided to go ahead with the testing, she was truly relaxed and not worried about the outcome.

Only the most gifted clairvoyant could have made the connection between the past incident and the current decision without interacting with the querent, asking cogent, compassionate questions, and truly listening to the answer. Yet even after I asked the question and listened, it still required some psychic ability to put it all together. The Influences layout turned out to be exactly the right reading; this querent was influenced by her past without even knowing it. (Note that the left side of an Influences reading is the influence you don't know about.)

The querent turned out to be fine. Her symptoms cleared up and she needed no further treatment.

Difficult Querents

Difficult querents are those who refuse to interact; they are closed off or distrustful, or they lie. I have encountered all of these and more as a tarot reader.

Querents Who Test and Lie

Querents sometimes want to test the reader. They want you to prove you are psychic and will withhold important facts in order to see if you can discern them on your own.

I once read cards for a stranger in a client-based setting (that is, she was a potential new client, getting her first reading). I used a Celtic Cross layout, and the Tower card covered her. I said, accurately, that she was losing her home. I also said that it seemed that the house was more than a house, that it was tied up with her sense of self. She said no to that, repeatedly. I asked her many different ways—saying that I saw this, that I was sure of it, but that I couldn't put my finger on it. She assured me, throughout a sixty-minute session, that this was not the case.

She was indeed losing her home. She was in the midst of a divorce, and the home was being sold to split the money between her and her ex. We discussed many of the things I saw in the cards, and yet she had an "I've got a secret" gleam in her eye the entire time.

As she was leaving, with her hand on the doorknob, she said, "I'm an interior decorator. The reason the home seems like it's an extension of me is because I decorated every bit of it myself." That was twenty-five years ago, and I'm still annoyed!

There's little you can do with a querent like this. Perhaps I should have told her flat out that holding back information was just taking away from her own experience. However, she could then have used my own statement as "evidence" that I wasn't a "real psychic." Indeed, *anything* that happened would have provided that evidence for her. After all, when I said that her home was tied up with how she saw herself, most people would have acknowledged that I had accurately guessed her career, without necessarily naming it. I once had a querent to whom I said that she worked with education and with the physical body—she was a gym teacher. A querent who was determined to test me and withhold from me could have concluded that because the words "gym teacher" didn't come from my mouth, I hadn't really gotten it!

Ultimately, if a querent wants to spend money to "prove" you're a fool, it's their money. Such people are rare and can frustrate your own sense of confidence and ability. As soon as possible after an encounter like that, give a reading to a friend or acquaintance you know to be receptive. It'll help you feel you have your mojo back!

Be honest with querents, and if it's not working, offer to give them their money back. Many are ambivalent about tarot: Is it real or is the reader a charlatan? Do I want to know my future or am I better off not knowing? Those mixed feelings can get mixed up into the cards and distort the reading.

If you feel your reading has become distorted, pick up the cards and shuffle like crazy, letting the shuffle feel like it is sloughing off the prior reading. Then lay out the cards again. If you do this, do a smaller reading. Let yourself focus, deeply, on just a few cards. Contrarily, if the first reading was small, lay additional cards on top of it. The idea is to change the playing field, shake things up, and move energy that feels stuck.

Querents Who Want What They Want

There was a guy in my town who was in a terrible relationship. He went to a reader, and she told him the relationship was a disaster. He went to another reader. And another. After he'd been to every reader he knew, he started over again from the beginning. He wanted someone to tell him to stay with that girl. No one would.

Everyone knows a version of this guy. He is seeking validation of his bad decision and will refuse to listen to any other answer.

There is only one solution when a querent like this seeks you out: refuse to do the reading.

Translators and Interpreters

If you're working with a translator or an interpreter, make sure that the querent makes eye contact with you. I've done readings of this kind several times, and have found myself in a situation where the querent starts talking to the translator instead of to me. This can prevent you from making a connection. I have found that readings with translators can be quite challenging for that reason.

Don't let the fact that you and the querent don't share a language be a barrier. Establish a connection by introducing yourself, getting the querent's name, shaking hands or giving a hug (as appropriate), and explaining what's happening. Maintain eye contact while listening to the querent's voice and intonation, and stay with the querent when hearing translation. If the querent ends up in a tete-a-tete conversation with the translator, break it up! Make sure they don't establish their own "language world" that excludes you.

Psychic Blocks

I worked once with a querent who told me sadly that she'd never been able to get a reading. Every time she tried, nothing happened; the information wasn't accurate, and the reading simply didn't touch her.

My reading with her went like this. I laid out the cards, and the first one didn't connect. The second didn't connect. The third didn't connect. The reading was dead.

I took a deep breath to let go of fear, to let the Psychic Child know we were okay.

"This isn't working," I said, washing the layout and pulling in all the cards.

"It never works for me," she said. "I've had readings before and this is what happens." She sounded sad. I felt immediately that this was about connection.

"Listen, we're going to do this. Look in my eyes and stay with me."

I shuffled the cards without breaking eye contact, and fanned them out on the table.

"Now let's stay in contact here." I placed my hands gently over hers, and asked her to pick a card from the fan. I read the card.

"Yes," she said.

We repeated the process. Eye contact. Hand contact. Slowly pick a card. Read it.

"Yes, that's true."

We read six cards that way—a small reading, but the process was slow. And powerful.

"That's all we're reading," I said. "You've broken through. There was a wall, but we broke it down together. You never again have to say that readings don't work for you. You can always break this wall."

This was a beautiful experience for both of us. We hugged. We had successfully used the cards to transcend a psychic block that had who-knows-what effect on her life. It was truly a healing.

Homework

Homework Questions

1. What are special considerations when reading for yourself?
2. What are special considerations when reading over the phone or via computer?
3. What are special considerations when reading for someone you know very well?
4. What are some things you can do if a reading feels "off"?

Homework Answers

1. If you're like me, when you care very much about an outcome, you may not be honest with yourself. This is a situation where you may reach out to another reader instead. Also, the tendency to read silently doesn't awaken the brain. Reading aloud will solve this.

2. The lack of eye contact (even Skype can be difficult) and the lack of touch—especially the lack of an ability for the querent

to touch the cards—can be challenges. You need to find alternative ways to visualize connection and create intimacy with your querent. For example, I allow my querents to tell me when to cut the cards.

3. There are two main concerns, the first being that you may know the querent so well that you make assumptions; you essentially give friendly advice rather than do a reading. The second concern is that you may hold back—either because the information is embarrassing, or because it's hard to give a loved one bad news.

4. First, acknowledge the problem. You'll do no good by faking it. In a worst-case scenario, offer a paying client his money back. Before that, try reshuffling the deck and laying out a small reading if you started with a larger layout. With a smaller layout, try adding more cards on top of the layout.

Exercises

Exercise: Charging for Readings

To charge or not to charge? This can be a difficult decision, because people have strong, often subconscious emotions about money.

Do this exercise when you are grounded and centered. Although a few cleansing breaths might be enough, consider a deeper meditation before you begin. You should be completely calm and feel connected to yourself.

1. Close your eyes and visualize charging for readings: You have regular clients, in person or over the phone. You make house calls, or they come to you, or it's entirely via phone and computer. Or you do your readings at Renaissance fairs and other public venues. Visualize whatever feels real to you. Don't just visualize *doing* the readings; visualize *being* a person who reads cards professionally, even if infrequently.

2. Write down everything you liked about the scenario(s) you envisioned. These "pros" (positive aspects) are personal to you, and are based on the experience of the visualization, not on something you decided rationally.

3. Now write down everything you disliked about charging for readings. Again, these "cons" should be personal and based on the feelings generated during the visualization.

4. Review your two lists. Are they about equal, or has a clear decision emerged? The simple process of list-making in a meditative state is a powerful tool for decision-making.

Of course, you could have skipped this exercise and simply done a reading. But reading for yourself is not for everyone, as discussed in this chapter. The next exercise will help you determine if reading your own cards is right for you.

Exercise: Being Your Own Querent

The results of this exercise will help you decide if you should read for yourself on serious matters or if you should go to another reader, perhaps trading readings, in order to see yourself more clearly.

This exercise adds a "hidden card" to your layouts. Use this card to learn what you are hiding from yourself.

1. Choose a layout you are comfortable with, one in this book (or not) or even one of your own. Determine the question you will ask. For the purpose of this exercise, it should not be a simple or silly reading, but something where you have some emotional energy invested in the outcome. "What movie should I see tonight?" is not the right sort of question, while "Should I propose to my girlfriend?" is. It can be a simple Yes/No layout or a more complex one, such as a Celtic Cross.

2. If you will use a significator, select it now.

3. Take several deep, cleansing breaths.

4. Shuffle or mix the cards, stopping when you feel it's right.

5. Do the reading as you normally would. Read out loud.

6. As a last card, take the bottom card from the unused portion of the deck and place it to the left of the layout. Read this card as "what I hide from myself." For example, illustration 49 shows the five-card Influences layout with the bottom card added to the left (hidden influences).

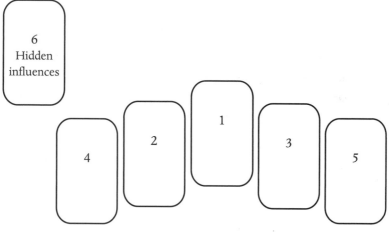

Illustration 49: What I Hide from Myself Spread

7. Make a note of this reading in your journal. Be sure to write down the following:

- Your question
- How you interpreted the reading before the hidden card appeared
- What changed after the hidden card appeared
- Your interpretation of the outcome

8. Repeat this exercise on a regular basis. Mark the pages in your journal where these readings appear so they are easy to find.

9. When real life has caught up with each reading and you know how the situation turned out, go back to your journal and determine the following things:

- Were you right overall?
- What did the hidden card say, and did that make the reading more accurate?
- How do you interpret the hidden card *now*, in hindsight?

Over a period of time, this exercise will teach you how much you hide from yourself, and how much that has an effect on the readings you do for yourself. The best possible outcome, if you want to read your own cards, is to discover that your readings proved accurate and the hidden card had little effect on the overall interpretation. On the other hand, you may discover that the hidden card has messages for you after the fact, and that rereading that card shows you exactly what you missed. If that's your pattern, then reading your own cards for serious issues is not something I recommend.

EIGHT

Interaction with Experimentation and Play

Most people use tarot cards in a very limited way. This chapter offers a variety of different ways to use them, ways that will loosen up your relationship with the cards and broaden your tarot horizons. By experimenting and playing with tarot cards, you will see previously unseen possibilities of what the cards can be in your life.

Tarot Experiments

People tend to use the tarot for two things: meditation and readings. Make that three things, since readings can be divided into predictive readings ("What will happen?") or therapeutic readings that function as a counseling session, with the cards as a medium of communication and insight. But there are plenty of other things to be done with a deck of cards!

There's no way I could offer every possible tarot experiment here; part of the point is for you to engage creatively with your own cards. What I can do, though, is give you some ideas of things I've done, things I've found effective, and allow them to inspire you.

Laying Cards on Things

Say you want to choose a baby name and just can't decide between two or three names. Or maybe it's not as serious as a baby name—maybe it's a pet name!

1. Write each name on a piece of paper or a sticky note.
2. If you want a "none of the above" option, also include a blank piece of paper.
3. Place the pieces of paper on a table before you.
4. Shuffle the deck while looking at the choices.
5. Lay one card on each choice.
6. Now read the cards. Maybe two of your three choices are reversed and one is upright: that makes it easy. If they're all upright, read the card meanings to make your decision. If they're all reversed, lay another card on each choice.

This example shows you how dropping a card onto something other than a layout can produce helpful results.

Cards can be dropped onto pictures, lists, maps, real estate listings, and so on. Your imagination is the only limitation here. You can lay pairs of cards and read the pair if that's more comfortable than a single-card reading. Whenever you're seeking a simple answer this way, pay close attention to reversals, but also pay attention to the angles and directions that we learned about in chapter 5. In the baby name example, is one card looking at one of the other card's names?

Following Cards

There are a number of ways to use tarot to help find lost objects, including this one:

1. Stand in the center of your room or in the center of your house.
2. Place a card in each of the four directions. You don't need a compass; in front of you, behind you, to your left, and to your right will do.

3. Look for indications as to which card to follow. If only one card is upright, go in that direction. If they're all reversed, lay out four more cards. Also look to see if any cards are pointing in a direction not their own. Decide where you're being led and go there. Bring your deck with you.

4. If you are now in another room and still can't find the object, lay out four more cards and continue to follow them.

This might be a job for a pendulum, for simplicity's sake, but tarot will work, too, and the experiment will give you an idea of the depths of exploration available with your deck.

Using Specific Cards for Guidance

Here's another way to find a lost object:

1. Again, stand in the center of your house or a room.

2. Start to lay out cards in a simple cross (illustration 50).

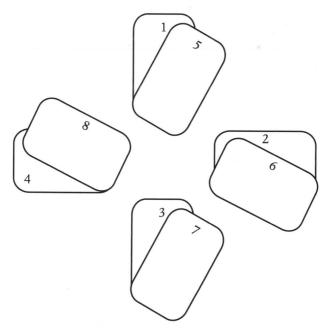

Illustration 50: Finding a Lost Object

3. Stop when you reach an ace. If the first card is an ace, you're done. If you have to keep going around and around through forty cards, so be it.

4. Once you reach an ace, walk in the direction in which the ace is pointing. So that means if the ace is reversed, go backward in your house, as if the ace is an arrow you are following. For example, if card 3 is an ace, go forward, toward the top of the layout; if it's reversed, go backward, toward the bottom.

This exercise assumes that the object is lost in your house, but you can also use a similar technique to find something (or someone) lost in a geographic region (a neighborhood, a town, a state). In this case, you can sit at a table and lay the cards out, then use a compass or map to determine where the ace is pointing.

Finding an ace is a common method of using the tarot to tell you something you need to know. Another is to seek a major arcana, or perhaps a specific suit or number. Finding a lost object is just one use for such a technique. You could also, for example, deal out cards on your baby name choices until a major turns up.

One thing these two lost-object exercises do is help you break free of always reading your cards while seated in one particular spot—on a table, under candlelight, or whatever. Cards on the floor as you follow their trail? Why not!

Lay cards wherever you desire. If you have a broken object (TV, car, dishwasher), you could lay three cards on it. Two or three upright cards means the object can be fixed, while two or three reversed means it must be replaced.

The idea here is to let the cards lay anywhere and everywhere they're needed.

Using Indicators on Cards

You can choose what color to paint the living room by cutting the deck and looking at the dominant color of the card.

I cut and got the Ace of Swords (illustration 51), so I guess the living room should be white.

Illustration 51: Robin Wood Ace of Swords

This may seem like the most trivial use of tarot cards imaginable, but I've presented it for two reasons: first, because the tarot connects to your intuition. In chapter 1, we talked about using the word "intuitive" to mean "psychic." In fact, they are two different things. You can have *both* abilities. While "psychic" tends to refer to things that you cannot know by conventional means (the future, the inside of someone else's heart), "intuitive" refers to things that are locked inside yourself.

Here is a very simple example. Somewhere within, you really do know exactly what color you want to paint the living room. Layered over that is a surface of indecision. It may be that the color you prefer doesn't seem like a good idea for some reason (it doesn't match the carpet?), or it may be that someone once told you that color was ugly, and that message is stuck somewhere in your subconscious, reverberating and causing doubt.

Perhaps the simple act of making this decision is difficult because you have issues with self-trust, or because when you were seven years old a teacher told you that you had no color sense at all and *that's* what's reverberating within, or because you've watched too many decorating shows and now it all seems like a very big and overwhelming deal. Whatever the reason, your indecision is like a curtain obscuring the clear window of what you really know and really want. Intuition is the ability to pull that curtain aside and just *know*, and tarot can help you access that intuitive knowledge.

Most of the time, pulling the curtain aside on painting the living room is the least of your concerns, but if you already have a relationship with the tarot, and it's really bothering you, why not use the tools at your disposal? More importantly, it's a good, straightforward example of the way you can use the cards to unlock an answer that you already know, or to access information that eludes you.

But I said there were two reasons I chose to include the paint-color example here. The other one is this: I didn't actually read the card. It didn't matter that I drew an ace or a sword; we weren't talking about the aggressive and forceful beginning of painting my living room. I simply drew a white card and keyed off of that.

This paint-color exercise is an easy-to-understand example of using other indicators on cards besides their designated meanings.

Finding a Missing Person

Somewhere around 1990, my then-husband met someone who was interested in starting a business with him. Isaac (my husband) had the know-how, and his acquaintance had the investment capital and was eager to get going.

And then, just as this man was about to sign the papers, his wife disappeared, locking him out of their shared bank accounts. He was in a total panic. (I have to say, my husband and I were not panicked. It wasn't our money. It was all pie in the sky at that point.) My husband told the man (I think his name was Peter, although I could be wrong— but we'll stick with that) that I was a psychic and perhaps could help.

I did a Celtic Cross layout for Peter. His marriage was definitely over; his wife had left him. (If I remember correctly, she'd fallen in love with someone else.) The cards showed anger and dissolution. It was a thorough reading, and it accurately revealed to Peter a bunch of information that he'd suspected and feared, but wasn't sure of and had been unable to find out.

Then he asked if I knew where she was.

The question momentarily stymied me—it's not the sort of thing that tarot is designed to answer. Having just read his cards for about forty-five minutes, I was feeling pretty tuned in, so I just looked at the cards for any geographical clues. It was safe to assume that the top of the layout was north, the right was east, and so on, and I began to look at it as if it were a map.

Illustration 52: Finding a Missing Person (Universal Tarot)

I was using the Waite-Smith deck. I don't remember every card, but I believe there was a Six and a Five of Swords (illustration 52). I said that she was near boats, and that water was to her west (note the water in the Five of Swords to the figure's left). He asked about mountains, their location relative to the water, and so on. Based on the information I provided, he successfully found her in Cape Cod (the water to the west proved to him she was on the Cape, and not the mainland).

Unfortunately, Peter's business deal was successfully quashed by his (soon-to-be-ex) wife's actions, but I had learned a powerful lesson about the cards.

To put it plainly, *everything* you see on a tarot card can be used.

Each of the cards that I used for geographical information had also been used (but meaning something else entirely) in the reading. The Six of Swords was a journey away from sorrow, as it generally is. But then I set aside those meanings, and read only the location imagery.

So far we've noted two things that appear on tarot cards separate from their specific meanings: color and location information. But there's far more than that, again, limited only by necessity and your imagination.

Tarot Affirmations

Lots of people include affirmations as part of their personal spiritual practice or as a psychological exercise. Tarot can be a part of that.

If you are using a tarot deck for affirmations, you might want a specific deck set aside for that purpose, apart from any deck you use for readings.

Choose a tarot card that represents something to which you aspire, and place it on your mirror or by your meditation space.

Remember that affirmations should always be *positive* and in the *present tense*. An affirmation is a statement of what you *are*.

For example, here's an affirmation using Temperance:

I am Temperance. I am balanced in all I do.

Generally, affirmations are repeated ten or twenty times. Do this while focusing your gaze on the Temperance card.

You might feel that Temperance has been achieved for now, or that the need for it is not as great. In that case, switch to another card.

You can also use a two-card combination, but affirmations should be simple, so don't use more than that.

A Tarot Wedding

When I got married in 2013, we decided to have a tarot-themed wedding. In addition to decorative tarot elements (including the invitations, cake topper, and centerpieces), my spouse and I created tarot-based wedding favors. It was an exercise in thinking outside the tarot box.

I created single-card interpretations for every guest. I took a deck, shuffled it, and laid out cards one by one. Sitting with the card, I wrote an interpretation (which is to say, I didn't go by the book—I gave a real single-card reading). Each interpretation was about 100 to 200 words in length.

In writing the interpretations, I had to be mindful that I didn't know which guest would receive which card. It might be someone who had never seen tarot before, or it might be someone who was a professional reader. It might even be a child (I decided everyone who was old enough to read should receive a reading).

I wrote the interpretations in a document that was later printed with a fancy font on parchment paper. (The document also included an explanation.) As I wrote, I was careful to keep the cards in order. I wrote only a few every night, for many weeks, and as I did so, the guest list was finalized and RSVPs came in, so I could get a more accurate count. In total, I ended up with 128 individual readings.

My spouse took the cards and the printout of readings and carefully placed each card and its reading in a blank envelope. She then shuffled the envelopes, with all the care and focus with which you shuffle cards before a reading.

Next we printed labels with the guests' names and table numbers (the envelopes served a dual purpose as place cards). Then we labeled every envelope.

Throughout the wedding, and afterward, guests told me how perfect their readings were; how it was the right message at the right moment. A few people asked me how I knew, and I had to explain that I didn't; that they had received a random card.

There were leftover favors, but we also received gifts from invited guests who couldn't attend. Those people received favors with their thank-you notes.

These wedding favors were my favorite experiment that I've ever performed with the tarot. Yes, they were readings, which is a conventional use for the cards. But everything about how the readings were done and how people received them was unconventional, and a creation unique to my wedding. Part of the joy of that day will always be the delight that the readings brought to our guests.

Exercise: Another List

1. Go back to the "Charging for Readings" exercise at the end of chapter 7. Split your list in two, so that "charge" and "don't charge" are on two separate sheets of paper.

2. Center yourself with a few deep, cleansing breaths.

3. Lay a pair of cards on each list.

4. Did this method illuminate the decision you made previously?

Exercise: What Else?

Come up with a list of other places you can place tarot cards. Keep the list in your journal, and add to it whenever an idea strikes you.

Some of the ideas might turn out to be awkward or unworkable. That's fine. Just keep an open mind.

Now make another list, this time of things you can see in cards besides the ones we discussed (location and color). This, too, should become part of your journal.

Tarot Games

When you learn tarot, you may sometimes feel rigid, like you have to follow all the rules you've been taught. Games are a great way to loosen up your interaction with the tarot, to get past the rigidity and rules. They allow you to have fun at the same time as you are improving your skills and broadening the kinds of interactions you can have with the cards. If you have a study group of other tarot students, games are a great way to interact within the group, breaking up serious study time with fun exercises.

Games can also forge connections between you and like-minded friends who may be open to the tarot but are not readers. Who knows? Sometimes these games might even create new readers! The following are tarot games I've enjoyed. All but the first are of my own invention.

Tarot Telephone

This is a solo game that my teacher, Susan, used to play all the time, although in truth, she didn't describe it as a game, just a habit. Keep in mind that Susan taught me tarot in the 1980s, when all telephones were land lines and they all had cords. The game works best if your phone is always in the same place.

How to Play
One Player

Keep a tarot deck by your phone. Whenever the phone rings, cut the deck to reveal a single card. Quickly predict the nature of the phone call, then answer the phone.

Tip: Keep a diary of your predictions and the outcomes.

Why It's a Good Game

You'll improve as a reader when you're forced to be quick and deft. It also helps your skill when you have immediate feedback as to your accuracy. Additionally, it's helpful that these quick, instant readings are about nothing serious at all, so you can relax and just let it happen. After all, who cares if you don't get "insurance salesman" right?

Tarot Bluff

This is a game that can be played with a group of friends. It's actually a great game for people with little to no experience reading the tarot, although it's fun for serious students as well. The game is based on Blind Man's Bluff Poker.

You can play with two people, but I think it's better with three or more. That way, each player hears multiple versions of his or her card.

How to Play

Three or More Players

Shuffle the deck and give everyone a card. Each person takes his own card, without looking at it, and holds it up to his forehead, face out. You'll now have a group of people seated in a circle, with tarot cards held up to their foreheads. Everyone can see every card except his or her own.

One person goes first. One at a time, all the other players briefly interpret the card held by the first player. The "blind" player then guesses what his own card is. Everyone gets a turn.

You can score for accurate guesses or just play for fun.

Why It's a Good Game

Everyone enjoys this game, which I've played many times. People learn a lot about how to read. I've played with mixed groups, some of whom know the tarot and some do not. Everyone can read in this playful and supportive environment, though, and even people who've never seen a deck of tarot cards before can interpret based on the picture they see and the feeling it evokes in them. The level playing field thus opens the psyche.

When I've played with people who didn't know how to read cards, they came up with interesting interpretations that the "blind" person (if experienced) was able to understand and use as a basis for guessing their own card. Because they didn't know the tarot, they weren't able to guess their own card based on listening to the descriptions that others gave them, but they had fun anyway. Being the "blind" person is a way to receive the wisdom of short readings in a playful way, and the inexperienced people enjoyed it as much as the advanced readers.

Playing this game also teaches you how to *listen*. Listening closely to what people tell you about the card you hold up is necessary if you're to guess accurately. Your listening skills will make you a better reader.

Zener Tarot

Zener cards are the ESP cards with circles, squares, squiggly lines, and so on. Zener cards were developed in the 1930s, based on the idea that the only way to truly test ESP is to be emotionally neutral—to offer symbols that in no way incite emotion. It was thought to be more scientific to eliminate emotion from parapsychology experiments.

But in the eighty or so years since Zener cards were designed, studies of psychic abilities (although few and far between) have suggested that strong emotion plays a role in triggering ESP. Since tarot cards have emotional content, they may be a better gauge of psychic ability.

This game replicates Zener psychic-skills testing, except using tarot cards. The one-player version tests clairvoyance (the ability to discern the future or the hidden present), and the two-player version tests telepathy (the ability to read what someone else is thinking). Both of these skills are useful in tarot reading.

How to Play

One-Player Version: Clairvoyance
Shuffle the deck and place one card face down before you. Take a few deep breaths and clear your mind. Visualize the card before you. Instead of trying to guess the card, write down your impressions. You may have the suit, the number, colors, other things visible on the card (mountains, fish, trees, people), a shape or direction, or perhaps a meaning. When you're ready, flip over the card and compare the results.

You might find you do better if you do several cards in a row before going back and flipping them over (be sure to retain the order).

Two-Player Version: Telepathy

Both players take deep, cleansing breaths to clear their minds. Make enough eye contact to establish a connection between the two of you. One player shuffles, draws a card, and looks at it, concentrating on its imagery. The other player writes down impressions, as in the clairvoyance version. When ready, the sender and receiver can review the receiver's notes together and compare them to the card. The sender can also talk about what he or she was thinking, and together, both players can determine if that influenced the receiver.

Again, you might try doing several cards in a row before reviewing the notes and then switching roles.

Why It's a Good Game

Everyone is fascinated by how "real" psychic abilities actually are, and here is a game that lets you explore that question.

While doing so, you're also creating strong emotional connections between images in your head and images on the card. You're learning your internal symbol system—what a picture in your head translates to in the real world.

Many people have these internal symbol systems without realizing it. These might be images; for example, when there are a lot of clouds in the sky on a tarot card, you visualize birds, even when there are no birds on the card. Or they might be physical or emotional impressions—I often *feel* water in my body when visualizing water/cups, even to the point of becoming aware of the saliva in my mouth or the tears in my eyes.

In addition, not everyone gets pictures. You might get sounds, words, bodily sensations, aromas, or simply thoughts, and all of these are valid forms of receiving psychic information. Playing psychic games allows you to become familiar with your personal psychic language.

Keyword Tarot

This is a cross between a Zener reading and a tarot reading, with some guessing game thrown in. The game is structured to be played with two people. If three or more people play, take turns being the pair doing the reading, going around a circle rather than back and forth.

How to Play

Two or More Players

If two people are playing, they will switch roles. If three or more play, choose two people to start.

Player 1 writes a single keyword on a piece of paper and folds the paper so the word is not visible. Keywords can be anything. Here are some samples: home, loss, poverty, wealth, job, travel, confusion, sex, anger, competition, play, friendship, alcoholism, exhaustion, busy, humor, baby, marriage, contentment.

Both players now take deep, cleansing breaths to clear their minds. Make enough eye contact to establish a connection between the two of you. Player 2 shuffles while player 1 concentrates on the keyword.

Player 2 draws a card and lays it on top of the paper containing player 1's keyword. This single card is intended to be an "answer" or "reading" for player 1's keyword.

Player 1 continues to concentrate on his or her keyword.

Now player 2 reads the card that he or she has placed upon player 1's keyword. (Although in other situations I recommend reading out loud to loosen up and empower the psyche, for purposes of a guessing game you should do it silently—otherwise player 1 may inadvertently indicate "hot" and "cold" with her facial expressions during the reading.)

Player 2 now writes down two or three keywords that arise as a result of the card. That is, player 2 considers the reading of the card and writes down two or three keywords that she feels best describe the card in this moment, in this reading.

Both players then reveal the keywords and see if there's a match.

If you want to keep score, give one point to player 2 if any of her keywords match player 1's keyword.

Then switch roles. If you're going around a circle, go to the next pair. Next time it comes back to these two players, they switch roles.

WHY IT'S A GOOD GAME

As with the previous games, Keyword Tarot gives you rapid feedback on your accuracy and forces you to get sharp with single-card readings. In addition, Keyword Tarot helps you improve your concentration skills and also helps you with communicating the meaning of tarot cards and your own interpretation of a reading. By forcing player 2 to use only two or three keywords, the game helps you develop simple explanations for what you see.

Conclusion

Together, through the pages of this interaction, we've been on quite a journey. We've explored statistics, art, and difficult people. We've learned and we've played.

Tarot is a lifetime study. For me, my greatest teachers have been the cards themselves and the querents with whom I've shared powerful, sometimes life-altering, readings. Books have been my friends, and I've studied many, but my hope with *Tarot Interactions* is that you'll be empowered to interact with the cards, the querents, and yourself in a way that will act as a greater teacher than any book possibly could.

I hope the education, and the interactions, are joyful for you.

Blessings,
Deborah Lipp

Appendix A:
Card Meanings

These meanings are based on Waite-Smith imagery and will apply to any deck based on it, including Robin Wood, Hanson-Roberts, Classic Tarot, and many more. You may find that in such Waite-Smith–based decks, one or a few cards have images (and perhaps therefore meanings) very different from those created by Arthur Edward Waite and Pamela Colman Smith, and you'll have to adapt your understanding to the deck being used.

Pentacles

Pentacles generally indicate money, career, or education. Pentacles correspond to the element of earth in the tarot.

Ace of Pentacles
UPRIGHT

All aces are beginnings. Here, the beginning is of a financial nature, perhaps a job, an investment, or a business.

REVERSED

A financial venture fails to get off the ground; a nonstarter.

Two of Pentacles
Upright
Keeping things in balance. The juggler must keep his balls in the air. I think of this card as "good" stress; joyfully, playfully doing the hard work that keeps a busy life going.

Reversed
"Bad" stress. In reverse, the juggler is overwhelmed, out of balance, and stressed.

Three of Pentacles
Upright
This card depicts a craftsman, skilled at what he does. In the Waite-Smith deck, he is working on the ornamentation over a doorway. The card represents talent at work, as well as recognition. The doorway suggests that the craftsman is "going somewhere."

Reversed
Hard work without (or without sufficient) recognition or reward.

Four of Pentacles
Upright
Miserliness, greed, grasping tightly to what you have and failing to see that you could have more.

Reversed
Letting money run through your fingers carelessly.

Five of Pentacles

UPRIGHT

Homelessness; loss of position or place. Being without a place in the world. Being without a spiritual home or any sense of well-being.

REVERSED

Temporary shelter. Finding a home or job or place, but it won't last; it's just a way station.

Six of Pentacles

UPRIGHT

This is a card of generosity; it can mean the querent receives a gift or help of some kind—there is a benefactor. This card often means a person (the benefactor), although it can also be read as a situation.

REVERSED

Gifts come with strings attached. The querent should beware of any loans or gifts because the real price might be too high. There may be shame associated with taking the gift.

Seven of Pentacles

UPRIGHT

Hard work; the will to create work, and satisfaction with the result. This is a card about the fruits of one's labor.

REVERSED

Reversed, the picture is the same: a person sees the results of his labor, but now he wonders if it was worth the trouble. The profit is just not commensurate with the effort required to earn it.

Eight of Pentacles

UPRIGHT

Educational or career progress. This card depicts a student excelling in his studies. Financial rewards will be small (the person is depicted as a student, not a master).

REVERSED

Laziness when approaching one's work or studies. Lack of attention to detail, or paying attention to the wrong details.

Nine of Pentacles

UPRIGHT

Satisfaction in being alone. When this card comes up in relation to questions of romance, the answer is generally that the querent will be alone but will learn to love being alone. Joy in the home and the garden. Connection to animals.

REVERSED

Minor disasters in the home, such as theft, intrusion, physical issues with the house, or other disruptions, such as legal issues.

Ten of Pentacles

UPRIGHT

All good things; a happy home, wealth, a loving family. Can also mean an inheritance or a family reunion. The person who receives this card can experience life's true fulfillment through family.

REVERSED

Disputes in the family, especially over money; perhaps a dispute over an inheritance.

Page of Pentacles
UPRIGHT

Pages tend to be young people or students. Here the page is focused on the concerns of pentacles—finance and stability. The page is someone who thinks about finances abstractly, and is perhaps more interested in economics than banking.

Pages are sometimes messages, so this card can be a message about a financial matter.

REVERSED

A lazy or disinterested young person. Someone who doesn't apply himself or is impractical.

Knight of Pentacles
UPRIGHT

A solid, salt-of-the-earth, dull, and practical young man. Perhaps an earth sign (Taurus, Capricorn, Virgo). In the Waite-Smith deck, the Knight of Pentacles is the only knight whose horse stands still. This man is stable and slow to act.

Knights can be the coming or going of a matter regarding the suit, so rapid movement regarding money or career might be indicated.

REVERSED

A stupid or stubborn person. Someone who obstructs. Someone bad with money.

Queen of Pentacles
UPRIGHT

This queen is sometimes seen as a kind of "mini-Empress"—loving, kind, fertile. Her downcast eyes in the Waite-Smith deck suggest moodiness or sorrow, but she is, by and large, a woman connected to fertility and nature. She has pets or children or, at least, a lush garden.

REVERSED

Infertility, mistrust, disconnection from nature and from one's inner nature.

King of Pentacles

Upright

A helpful person associated with money—a banker or loan officer, or a friend or relative able to provide concrete, tangible assistance, especially money. An older (over thirty) man or a worldly man is generally indicated.

Reversed

The same sort of person is unhelpful, withholds money, or prevents the querent from succeeding financially.

Swords

Swords are concerned with aggression, conflict, speech, argument, or intense movement. In most tarot decks, swords correspond to the element of air, although in some decks, swords are fire.

Ace of Swords

UPRIGHT

A beginning related to swords; an especially aggressive or sudden new event in one's life.

REVERSED

A new venture doesn't get off the ground because you're using too much force. Let it happen; don't force it.

Two of Swords

UPRIGHT

Stasis; waiting for something to happen before taking any further steps. A stalemate.

REVERSED

The end of a period of waiting, with a suggestion of unwise action—the danger that caused the original stalemate is still out there.

Three of Swords

UPRIGHT

Sorrow. Heartbreak.

REVERSED

The end of sorrow. Sorrow is in the recent past; healing has begun, but wounds are still there.

Four of Swords
UPRIGHT

Withdrawal from the material world; a much-needed period of rest and/or contemplation.

REVERSED

The period of rest and reclusion has ended. There is an eagerness to reengage with the world. Keep your eyes open to what you missed while you were gone.

Five of Swords
UPRIGHT

Theft; deception; a combat that leaves everyone (victor and vanquished) worse off than they were before.

REVERSED

An empty or Pyrrhic victory.

Six of Swords
UPRIGHT

A journey away from sorrow. Escape into a new place or situation.

REVERSED

A journey cannot be undertaken. There is no escape.

Seven of Swords
UPRIGHT

A theft or deception; a dissolute and dishonest will. A spy, trickery, a sneak-thief.

REVERSED

The enemy is disarmed, so the battle is avoided. What was lost is returned.

Eight of Swords

UPRIGHT

A trap; no progress is possible; weakness; imprisonment. Hold still, because you don't know what's out there.

REVERSED

The end of an illness or an abusive situation. Getting your sea legs back after an illness can be difficult. Release from fear or imprisonment.

Nine of Swords

UPRIGHT

Depression, grief, loss.

REVERSED

The end of mourning. Rising up from one's bed after a long illness.

Ten of Swords

UPRIGHT

Utter defeat.

REVERSED

Recovery from defeat; life can begin again.

Page of Swords

UPRIGHT

An agile young person. A dancer. A student of ideas, language, or dance. Perhaps a spy.

REVERSED

Glibness, deception, or dishonesty. A spy is exposed.

Knight of Swords

UPRIGHT

An aggressive, forceful young man. Rapid movement. Someone hot-tempered and impulsive.

REVERSED

A dangerously angry person, possibly an abuser. Arguments, perhaps violence.

Queen of Swords

UPRIGHT

A smart, verbal woman; a leader. Someone sharp, perceptive, tough. Perhaps a widow.

REVERSED

A woman with a cruel tongue. Someone nasty, cutting. Abortion or miscarriage.

King of Swords

UPRIGHT

A fair-minded, mature man. A judge or lawyer or someone making a decision that affects the querent.

REVERSED

A severe, judgmental man. Someone more interested in being right than in achieving true justice.

Wands

Wands indicate building, creating, establishing, or labor. A career-oriented card in the suit of wands is generally about establishing oneself rather than about one's earning potential. In most tarot decks, wands are connected to the element of fire, although in a few, wands are air.

Ace of Wands
UPRIGHT

The beginning of an endeavor related to wands—creating or building something. The Ace of Wands can also be phallic and represent a sexual beginning.

REVERSED

A planned project fails to take off. A beginning falls through.

Two of Wands
UPRIGHT

Waiting for news about an opportunity. Pinning one's hopes on something, particularly a business, creative, or scientific venture.

REVERSED

The opportunity may not come through, but you're fine anyway. In many decks, the Two of Wands shows someone wearing rich clothing; remind the querent that the opportunity was extra, and not a necessity.

Three of Wands
UPRIGHT

Waiting for an opportunity; a partnership in the offing. Good connections can turn things around.

REVERSED

Waiting and waiting for something that will never arrive.

Four of Wands
UPRIGHT

A wedding; a celebration; joyous connections.

REVERSED

Happiness in small things. Appreciate small joys in life; family, simplicity, and get-togethers.

Five of Wands
UPRIGHT

Combat, but playful. You know it's all a game. Happy competition.

REVERSED

You've forgotten it's a game. Suddenly, competition seems deadly serious. Danger.

Six of Wands
UPRIGHT

Acknowledgment of success, rewards, and praise, as well as a potential journey. A journey that leads to success.

REVERSED

The journey forestalled. A planned trip will not happen. No one notices the work you've done. Success goes unrewarded.

Seven of Wands
UPRIGHT

The will to succeed, fight back, and win. The querent is embattled and outnumbered, but can easily win because he has high ground.

REVERSED

A failure to plan; the querent hasn't taken high ground and is unprepared. Being overwhelmed by enemies.

Eight of Wands

UPRIGHT

Rapid forward movement. Messages received or sent about a rapidly changing matter. Arrows of love.

REVERSED

The message has not been received. Arrows of jealousy.

Nine of Wands

UPRIGHT

Cautious, guarded: the person depicted in the Waite-Smith deck is wounded and on guard. This indicates that the caution is warranted—he's already been wounded once and is protecting himself from further attack. Maybe over-cautious; perhaps he's blocking out love or kindness in his efforts at self-protection.

REVERSED

Unaware, unguarded. Letting one's guard down. Gullible; naive; the querent may be opening himself up to injury or attack.

Ten of Wands

UPRIGHT

Carrying a tremendous burden without help. Overwhelmed; exhausted; at the edge of failure.

REVERSED

Forcing one's burden unfairly or cruelly upon others.

Page of Wands
UPRIGHT

A young person interested in wand concerns. A message, or a messenger. A "fair-haired boy" in the sense of being favored or lucky (regardless of whether this person is fair-haired or male) having charisma, charm, and a charmed life.

REVERSED

An unpleasant message. A theatrical, dramatic, or unstable person. A "red-headed stepchild" who doesn't fit in.

Knight of Wands
UPRIGHT

A passionate man who brings fire into one's life. Playful and spontaneous. The rapid coming or going of a matter related to wand concerns.

REVERSED

Heedless, self-centered, concerned only with his own needs, the Knight of Wands reversed can also be jealous and vain.

Queen of Wands

UPRIGHT

A woman who is warm and easygoing but perhaps shy; a homebody. A good cook.

REVERSED

A woman who rules her domain with an iron fist. Strict, even severe. Perhaps unfaithful.

King of Wands

UPRIGHT

An older (over thirty) man, usually a family man. He is fair, focused, and intense, with the passions of fire. He might have a profession related to wands (construction, entrepreneurship).

REVERSED

Rigid in his opinions, the King of Wands reversed likes the rules better than their purpose. Can be bigoted.

Cups

Cups are about love, emotions, memory, dreams, or the subconscious. They correspond to the element of water.

Ace of Cups
UPRIGHT

The beginning of love.

REVERSED

The romance will not happen.

Two of Cups
UPRIGHT

A meeting of minds. A couple connected emotionally, mentally, and in every way. A wonderful romance or close friendship.

REVERSED

A breakup or disruption in a romance. A misunderstanding in an important relationship.

Three of Cups
UPRIGHT

Joyful social connection. Friends and relationships are especially important now. Parties, socializing.

REVERSED

Parties turned sour. Drunkenness, gossip, the wrong kind of socializing.

Four of Cups
Upright

Someone who hates what he has, without realizing there is something even better available. Questioning the material world, wondering if there is more, but not really looking for more, just looking at one's own discontent.

Reversed

Someone who embraces the possible. The person sees the spiritual as well as the material, sees what may be hoped for as well as what is already present, and embraces the blessings life offers.

Five of Cups
Upright

Grieving over a loss even though you still have plenty. The person feels bereft but has not lost everything. This card typically depicts a person looking at three spilled cups, while two full cups are behind him, out of view. He hasn't lost everything; he just thinks he has, and can change his attitude if he chooses.

Reversed

Here the person focuses on the two full cups. Aware of what he has lost, he still has hope.

Six of Cups
Upright

Nostalgia, a reminder of the past. A reunion—usually sweet—with someone from long ago; something from childhood returns.

Reversed

Here, the past is a trap; someone from the past brings bad news or a betrayal; nostalgia can be poisonous.

Seven of Cups

UPRIGHT

Sevens relate to will, and here we see a dissipated and confused will; the inability to apply will is suggested. The querent has a wide array of choices and cannot decide which is correct.

REVERSED

Inability to make a decision. The best choice is to make any choice; even a wrong one will break this paralysis.

Eight of Cups

UPRIGHT

The Waite-Smith deck depicts a person stacking up all his possessions (cups) and walking away, seeking wisdom. The image suggests leaving something behind, even though it's still good, for a higher level of some kind. The querent knows that one's material possessions are not what's important in life. There may also be a real dissatisfaction with what one already has. A life change.

REVERSED

Leaping back into one's life; embracing what one has. Rejecting the lofty or ascetic in favor of pleasure.

Nine of Cups

UPRIGHT

The Nine of Cups is known as the "wish card." Upright, you get your wish.

REVERSED

In reverse, your wish is not granted.

Ten of Cups
UPRIGHT

This is a card of all good things. Loving family; deep, emotionally satisfying connections; enough of everything.

REVERSED

Discord, misunderstanding, the breakup of a once-happy home.

Page of Cups
UPRIGHT

A thoughtful young person; someone seeking wisdom. A lover of poetry, stories, and storytelling. A dreamer. A message regarding these things.

REVERSED

A wasteful, spoiled, or bratty young person. Problems with one's studies.

Knight of Cups
UPRIGHT

A man bringing love or a loving message into one's life. A Prince Charming.

REVERSED

The Prince is not what he seems; an unfaithful lover, a false friend.

Queen of Cups
UPRIGHT

An enticing, beautiful, and moody woman. In the Waite-Smith deck, hers is the only covered cup, indicating hidden feelings, closely guarded. She is secretive and vulnerable.

REVERSED

Depression or mental illness. Emotions are arbitrary and treacherous. A woman who may mean well but has no self-control.

King of Cups
UPRIGHT

A wise counselor; often a psychiatrist or psychologist or other person in the helping professions. His own emotions aren't shared; he is concerned with the emotions of others.

REVERSED

An emotionally manipulative person, possibly an abuser. He is guarded and secretive, to the detriment of the querent.

The Major Arcana

Major arcana indicate that large forces are at play. These are cards of fate, of God or Spirit working in our lives, and of life-changing events. Often, major arcana speak of the querent's spiritual state or of deep lessons to be learned.

0. *The Fool*

UPRIGHT

The Fool makes a heedless choice that transforms him utterly. Usually depicted as on the verge of stepping off a cliff, he represents the cliff one could step off that would change one's life. It's doing the thing that everyone says is crazy, "damn the torpedoes," going for broke; being insanely, wonderfully daring and foolish. This card advises the querent to take the risk, to allow himself to be considered a fool.

REVERSED

In reverse, true foolishness is indicated; someone (perhaps the querent) is acting like an idiot and endangering himself and/or those around him.

1. *The Magician*

UPRIGHT

A person (often a man) of considerable personal ability. He's the "whole package." The altar before him has the four tools of the tarot, indicating he has equal power over all aspects of life. Creative power; the potential to begin anything.

REVERSED

Misuse of power; power used for unsavory ends. Waste of power.

2. The High Priestess
UPRIGHT

Mystery, the unknown, secrets, wisdom. Perhaps initiation of some kind, if the querent is on, or considering, a path that includes that. A mysterious and wise woman.

REVERSED

The opposite of wisdom. Staying on the surface and avoiding the deeper truth. Gossip and spite.

3. The Empress
UPRIGHT

Fertility in all endeavors (creative, financial, physical). A strong possibility of pregnancy. Generosity. Marriage.

REVERSED

Infertility. Nothing can grow. Stagnation. Poverty.

4. The Emperor
UPRIGHT

Mastery over the material world; authority, power. A wise ruler.

REVERSED

A weak ruler, one who "lets the inmates rule the asylum." Lack of self-control.

5. The Hierophant
UPRIGHT

Authority, cultural norms, conformity. Unwillingness to change. Conservatism.

REVERSED

Rebellion against authority. Rejection of conventional wisdom. Seeking one's own path.

6. *The Lovers*

UPRIGHT

Love, romance, a good match. A choice between what you want impulsively and what you know is right.

REVERSED

A bad choice. A romance turned sour. Arguments in a relationship.

7. *The Chariot*

UPRIGHT

Control, mastery, the need to maintain strict control to prevent chaos. The charioteer holds powerful horses in check who would otherwise run wild. A strong will holds things together.

REVERSED

An out-of-control person or situation. The horses, rather than the charioteer, drive the chariot. Holding on for dear life.

8. *Strength*

UPRIGHT

The power of compassion. Most decks depict a woman petting a lion, showing that strength comes from kindness rather than brute force. (If you're using a deck that shows a wrestler or Hercules, then you would interpret this card as a more conventional meaning of "strength.") Spiritual strength through love rather than force.

REVERSED

Brute force. Trying to bully or force your will onto a situation. Domination.

9. *The Hermit*

UPRIGHT

Seeking wisdom from a wise teacher. Alternately, seeking wisdom in isolation; removing oneself from society in order to look inward.

REVERSED

A reversal of the two upright meanings: either leaving a "hermitage" (ending a period of isolation) and reentering the world, or rejecting the advice of a guru or teacher; refusing to learn.

10. *Wheel of Fortune*

UPRIGHT

The Wheel turns in a fortunate way. Good luck. Your fate is not in your control, but you're lucky for now. Count your blessings and don't count on things staying stable. What goes around comes around.

REVERSED

Bad luck; nothing good will come of the current plans. Things won't go your way no matter what you do.

11. *Justice*

UPRIGHT

A legal matter; the involvement of judges, lawyers, or courts. Fairness, justice. A decision in the querent's favor.

REVERSED

Injustice. Unfairness. A decision against the querent.

12. *The Hanged Man*

UPRIGHT

Wisdom gained through suffering or an ordeal. Most decks depict a man in meditation while hanging upside down, indicating that enlightenment and the next level will only be achieved by undergoing a difficult experience.

REVERSED

Unwillingness to face the hard work needed in order to achieve a goal; laziness; taking the easy way out. The querent isn't going anywhere because he isn't doing the work needed to get there.

13. *Death*

UPRIGHT

Transformation, change. A new state of being. Rebirth.

REVERSED

Everything will stay the same. Stagnation.

14. *Temperance*

UPRIGHT

Inner balance. Spiritual and material, work and play, inner life and outer life—all are in balance.

REVERSED

Imbalance. Alcoholism. Self-indulgence. A life out of control.

15. The Devil
UPRIGHT

A prison of one's own making. The Waite-Smith deck depicts a couple chained, but loosely; they could free themselves but do not. Their own desires keep them trapped. Greed, alcoholism or addiction, infidelity—any "temptation" might be the chain that keeps one bound to the Devil.

REVERSED

Freeing oneself from the prisons that have bound one. The beginnings of freedom from evil.

16. The Tower
UPRIGHT

Utter disaster; a loss of great magnitude, especially a material loss. Losing one's home. A crime is uncovered.

REVERSED

Disaster on a small scale. Minor chaos in the home. A break-in or theft; petty crime.

17. The Star
UPRIGHT

Physical, psychological, and spiritual well-being. Health. Balance.

REVERSED

General ill health, in body, mind, or spirit. A health crisis. Disconnection from the self or one's spiritual nature. Pessimism and darkness.

18. The Moon
UPRIGHT

Mystery, deception, intuition, dreams. The unknown intrudes into the querent's life. The querent is lost, confused.

REVERSED

A mystery is revealed. Answers the querent sought are now apparent. A secret is uncovered. Tread lightly; there is still risk.

19. The Sun
UPRIGHT

A successful journey; an adventure into the unknown. The child/Sun leaves the flower garden and ventures into the wide world; the bright sunlight follows him, indicating hope and blessings. The present situation is safe and comfortable but childlike; the card indicates a willingness to move beyond the safe walls of childhood and venture into adulthood. Joy is within.

REVERSED

Playing it safe. Staying protected and avoiding venturing beyond one's known limits. Fearfulness. Refusing to grow up.

20. Judgement
UPRIGHT

Rebirth; a spiritual uplifting. Often, this card depicts the Resurrection, and indicates a deepened spiritual awareness. Good things coming. Good health.

REVERSED

No interest in the spiritual side of things. Refusal to change. Fear of change, fear of death, fear of the unknown. Poor health.

21. *The World*

Upright

All good things; a well-rounded success that is both material/financial and emotionally rich. Fulfillment of desires; good luck; rewards.

Reversed

Loss of possessions, both material and spiritual. Loss of position or rank. Can also be the refusal to learn lessons from life.

Appendix B: Patterns

Suits

Swords: A pattern of swords indicates that the reading has a lot to do with aggression, conflict, speech, or argument, or that there is intense movement related to the reading.

Wands: A pattern of wands indicates that the reading has a lot to do with building, creating, establishing, or labor.

Cups: A pattern of cups indicates that the reading has a lot to do with love, emotions, or the subconscious.

Pentacles: A pattern of pentacles indicates that the reading has a lot to do with money, career, or education.

Court Cards

A pattern of court cards suggests that there are a lot of people around, and that people, socializing, and/or one's social or family life figure importantly in the reading. A reading with a lot of court cards is not inwardly focused. Others matter a great deal, whether those others are welcome or not.

Pages: Students, young people, messages, the element of air.

The Page of Swords is the airy quality of air, or swords, or sword-related matters. The Page of Wands is the airy quality of fire, wands, or wand-related matters. The Page of Cups is the airy quality of water, cups, or cups-related matters. The Page of Pentacles is the airy quality of earth, pentacles, or pentacle-related matters.

Knights: Young men; the coming or going of a matter; the element of fire (fire of air, fire of fire, etc., following the same pattern described under Pages).

Queens: Women, mother, the element of water.

Kings: Mature men, father, the element of earth.

Major Arcana

A preponderance of major arcana indicates that large forces are at play. The querent may have little control over the events that are unfolding. A lot of majors in a reading may indicate the following:

- The subjects depicted in the reading are life-changing events that will affect the querent for years to come.
- The querent may have little control over the outcome; the matter may be in the hands of fate.
- The querent is at a crossroads; decisions made now will determine the querent's future.
- The cards may indicate life lessons that must be learned.

By contrast, an absence of majors can indicate that the events are just ordinary life events, and are no big deal in the grand scheme of things.

Numbers

Ace—Keyword: *Beginning*

Two—Keywords: *Balance, duality, stasis*

Three—Keywords: *Outcome, triangle, flux*

Four—Keywords: *Possession, stability, reality, result*

Five—Keyword: *Change*

Six—Keyword: *Journey*

Seven—Keywords: *Willpower, self-control*

Eight—Keywords: *Progress, strength*

Nine—Keyword: *Fulfillment*

Ten—Keyword: *Completion*

Appendix C: Recommended Reading

The following are books I recommend for students wishing to further their studies. It's not a long or exhaustive list, and it's not "the best" list. It's just a list of books I'm fond of, that have helped me or piqued my interest, and that I think you'll like as well. An alphabetical list with full details can be found in the bibliography.

Books That Aren't About Tarot

In chapter 1, I strongly urged you to take up a meditation practice. I have a favorite book on the subject, one I recommend above all others:

Meditation: The Complete Guide by Patricia Monaghan and Eleanor
G. Viereck

This outstanding book presents many different schools and styles—Eastern and Western—of meditation. Most books simply teach the technique in which the author has expertise, be it loving-kindness or zazen. This book gives you the world tour. If you've struggled with meditation, this may open your eyes to a different way.

In chapter 2, we discussed a variety of other esoteric disciplines, and I offered exercises connected to pathworking. If this is something you'd like to explore, I recommend these two books:

Magical Pathworking: Techniques of Active Imagination by Nick Farrell

The Initiate's Book of Pathworkings: A Bridge of Dreams by Dolores Ashcroft-Nowicki

Ashcroft-Nowicki, in particular, is a renowned expert on the topic.

General Books on the Tarot

Mastering the Tarot by Eden Gray

You must have anticipated that I'd recommend this one! If I had started my tarot studies with Arthur Edward Waite's *The Pictorial Key to the Tarot* (which is in the public domain and can be downloaded to your mobile device for free), I might have given up. It's dense and esoteric, and the turn-of-the-century writing style would have been off-putting when I was twenty-one. (It has grown on me.)

Eden Gray's book has deep esoteric knowledge, but it reads as if it doesn't. You can flip through it for quick-and-dirty card meanings, and if that's all you want, you'll be very satisfied indeed. Underneath, though, there's a quiet wisdom. This book has been my companion for thirty years.

Dictionary of the Tarot by Bill Butler

Tarot Dictionary and Compendium by Jana Riley

Bill Butler's book is one of the first I owned on the subject, and I adore it, but it can be hard to find. Riley's is similar and in print as of this writing.

These books compile interpretations from multiple experts on the tarot, and offer views of multiple card decks. Riley adds things like correspondences to gems, colors, and astrology. The idea is to broaden your view. There's something profound and freeing about reading experts who contradict one another, and experiencing the great variety that tarot has to offer.

Seventy-Eight Degrees of Wisdom: A Book of Tarot by Rachel Pollack

The New Tarot Handbook: Master the Meanings of the Cards by Rachel Pollack

The lazy way to write this recommended reading section would be to tell you, "Just buy stuff by Rachel Pollack." She's written quite a lot on the subject and it's all excellent. *Seventy-Eight Degrees of Wisdom* is considered by many to be *the* book on the subject, providing perhaps the deepest card-by-card analysis of the Waite-Smith deck available. It's a book that taught me whole new ways of being observant. *The New Tarot Handbook* is Pollack's version of Eden Gray's classic (by her own admission!). It's a shorter, more direct and accessible book (although you should still get *Seventy-Eight Degrees*).

Robin Wood Tarot: The Book by Robin Wood

Most companion books (books written to accompany tarot decks) are pretty lightweight. Card meanings are often no more than a few words, and are often derivative of other works. Sometimes they explain the specific or unusual illustration of the deck they accompany, but don't have any universal applicability.

Robin Wood is different. First, it's one of my favorite decks, one I use quite often, as you've noticed in these pages. But the book would be a wonderful addition to the library of someone reading with a different deck entirely. Wood's straightforward, direct, and humorous style is easy to read, but doesn't diminish her depth of understanding. In fact, I think the personality conveyed in this book goes a long way toward explaining why I love the deck, which is equally straightforward and deep. The book explores symbols, offers keywords, and really lets the reader in on the experience of creating a tarot deck as well as using it often.

Specialized Books on the Tarot

I'm a big fan of tarot author Mary K. Greer. She's serious about the subject, has a great depth of knowledge, and has been writing on the topic for a very long time. She's written two books on specialized subjects that cause confusion to many readers, and I recommend them both:

The Complete Book of Tarot Reversals by Mary K. Greer

Understanding the Tarot Court by Mary K. Greer and Tom Little

Chapter 4 covered tarot layouts, including creating your own layout. Since that's a pretty complex subject and we only covered it briefly, I recommend a couple of books for those of you who wish to explore layout creation in depth:

Tarot Spreads: Layouts & Techniques to Empower Your Readings by Barbara Moore

Tarot: Get the Whole Story: Use, Create & Interpret Tarot Spreads by James Ricklef

In chapter 7, we talked about reading professionally—whether and how much to charge, and whether professional reading is right for you. If this is a topic you wish to explore, I recommend this book:

Professional Tarot: The Business of Reading, Consulting, and Teaching by Christine Jette

Multi-Disciplinary Books

In chapter 2, I talked about how you might blend other esoteric disciplines with the tarot. So the following three books, which do just that, are of particular interest. They combine tarot with astrology, with Kabbalah, and with Jungian psychology. This is just a sampling of multi-disciplinary reading. Jung himself was fascinated by the tarot, so the Jungian work can support a really deep dive. Many Kabbalists work with tarot, as do astrologers (in chapter 5, I even talked about my tarot client who is an astrologer).

Blending Astrology, Numerology, and the Tarot by Doris Chase Doane

The Fool's Pilgrimage: Kabbalistic Meditations on the Tarot by Stephan A. Hoeller

Jung and Tarot: An Archetypal Journey by Sallie Nichols

Bibliography

Ashcroft-Nowicki, Dolores, with Tamara Ashcroft-Nowicki. *The Initiate's Book of Pathworkings: A Bridge of Dreams*. York Beach, ME: Samuel Weiser, 1999.

Butler, Bill. *Dictionary of the Tarot*. New York: Schocken Books, 1975.

Doane, Doris Chase. *Blending Astrology, Numerology, and the Tarot*. Tempe, AZ: American Federation of Astrologers, 2012.

Farrell, Nick. *Magical Pathworking: Techniques of Active Imagination*. St. Paul, MN: Llewellyn Publications, 2004.

Gray, Eden. *Mastering the Tarot: Basic Lessons in an Ancient Mystic Art*. New York: Signet Books, 1973.

Greer, Mary K. *The Complete Book of Tarot Reversals*. St. Paul, MN: Llewellyn Publications, 2002.

Greer, Mary K., and Tom Little. *Understanding the Tarot Court*. St. Paul, MN: Llewellyn Publications, 2004.

Hoeller, Stephan A. *The Fool's Pilgrimage: Kabbalistic Meditations on the Tarot*. Wheaton, IL: Quest Books/Theosophical Publishing House, 2004. Originally published as *The Royal Road*. Wheaton, IL: Theosophical Publishing House, 1975.

Jette, Christine. *Professional Tarot: The Business of Reading, Consulting, and Teaching.* St. Paul, MN: Llewellyn Publications, 2003.

Monaghan, Patricia, and Eleanor G. Viereck. *Meditation: The Complete Guide.* Novato, CA: New World Library, 1999.

Moore, Barbara. *Tarot Spreads: Layouts & Techniques to Empower Your Readings.* Woodbury, MN: Llewellyn Publications, 2012.

Nichols, Sallie. *Jung and Tarot: An Archetypal Journey.* York Beach, ME: Weiser Books, 1980.

Pollack, Rachel. *The New Tarot Handbook: Master the Meanings of the Cards.* Woodbury, MN: Llewellyn Publications, 2012.

———. *Seventy-Eight Degrees of Wisdom: A Book of Tarot.* Revised. New York: Thorson's Publishing, 1997.

Ricklef, James. *Tarot: Get the Whole Story: Use, Create & Interpret Tarot Spreads.* St. Paul, MN: Llewellyn Publications, 2004.

Riley, Jana. *Tarot Dictionary and Compendium.* San Francisco, CA: Red Wheel/Weiser, 1995.

Wood, Robin. *Robin Wood Tarot: The Book.* Dearborn, MI: Livingtree Books, 1998.

Art Credits

Anna.K Tarot, printed by Llewellyn Worldwide Ltd., used with permission.

Elisabeth Alba, illustrations on pages 94–95, 121–122.

Gilded Tarot, artwork by Ciro Marchetti, printed by Llewellyn Worldwide Ltd., used with permission.

Llewellyn's Classic Tarot, artwork by Eugene Smith, printed by Llewellyn Worldwide Ltd., used with permission.

Medieval Tarot, artwork by Guido Zibordi Marchesi, printed by Lo Scarabeo, used with permission.

Robin Wood Tarot, printed by Llewellyn Worldwide Ltd., used with permission.

Tarot Art Nouveau, Pietro Alligo and Antonella Castelli, artwork by Antonella Castelli, printed by Lo Scarabeo, used with permission.

Tarot Illuminati, artwork by Erik C. Dunne, printed by Lo Scarabeo, used with permission.

Universal Tarot, artwork by Roberto De Angelis, printed by Lo Scarabeo, used with permission.

To Write to the Author

If you wish to contact the author or would like more information about this book, please write to the author in care of Llewellyn Worldwide Ltd. and we will forward your request. Both the author and publisher appreciate hearing from you and learning of your enjoyment of this book and how it has helped you. Llewellyn Worldwide Ltd. cannot guarantee that every letter written to the author can be answered, but all will be forwarded. Please write to:

Deborah Lipp
℅ Llewellyn Worldwide
2143 Wooddale Drive
Woodbury, MN 55125-2989

Please enclose a self-addressed stamped envelope for reply,
or $1.00 to cover costs. If outside the U.S.A., enclose
an international postal reply coupon.

Many of Llewellyn's authors have websites with additional information and resources. For more information, please visit our website at http://www.llewellyn.com.

Visit us online to browse hundreds of our books and decks, plus sign up to receive our e-newsletters and exclusive online offers.

- **• Free tarot readings • Spell-a-Day • Moon phases**
- **• Recipes, spells, and tips • Blogs • Encyclopedia**
- **• Author interviews, articles, and upcoming events**

MASTER THE MEANINGS OF THE CARDS

The New Tarot
HANDBOOK

RACHEL POLLACK

The New Tarot Handbook
Master the Meanings of the Cards
RACHEL POLLACK

Renowned tarot author Rachel Pollack presents a book that shares tarot's vast and wonderful storehouse of wisdom and secrets in a direct, accessible way. Not only will readers learn what each card signifies, but more importantly, they will discover how to look at a tarot card and find their own truth. Using this guide, even complete beginners can immediately begin to do tarot readings—yet the book's richness and depth will invite them back again and again to discover even greater levels of wisdom within its pages.

978-0-7387-3190-2, 288 pp., 5 ³/₁₆ x 8   **$15.95**

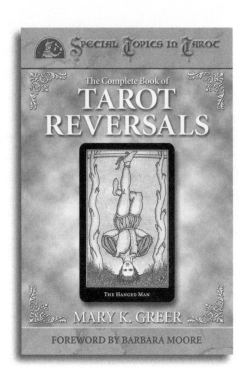

SPECIAL TOPICS IN TAROT

The Complete Book of

TAROT
REVERSALS

THE HANGED MAN

MARY K. GREER

FOREWORD BY BARBARA MOORE

The Complete Book of Tarot Reversals

MARY K. GREER

What do you do with the "other half" of the Tarot deck: the reversed cards? Experienced and beginning Tarot readers alike often struggle with interpreting cards when they're upside down.

Struggle in the dark no more. Respected Tarot scholar and author Mary K. Greer sheds light on the subject in *Tarot Reversals*, the first book in Llewellyn's *Special Topics in Tarot* series. This series was created in response to an increasing demand for more Tarot books on advanced and specialized topics.

Reversals are not black and white—there is more than one way to interpret them. Explore these shades of gray with twelve different methods for reading upside-down cards. Upright and reversed interpretations for each of the 78 cards offer inner support, positive advice, and descriptions of the learning opportunities available, yet with a twist that is uniquely their own. Stimulate your intuition and deepen your connection to the cards as you explore the flip side of the Tarot.

978-1-56718-285-9 288 pp., 6 x 9   **$16.95**

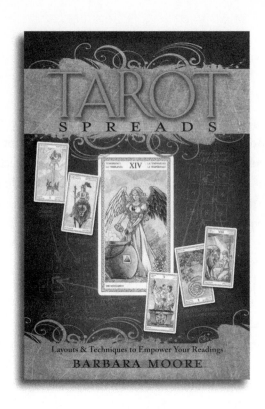

TAROT
S P R E A D S

Layouts & Techniques to Empower Your Readings

BARBARA MOORE

Tarot Spreads
Layouts & Techniques to Empower Your Readings
Barbara Moore

Add power, precision, and depth to your tarot readings—this friendly guide tells you how to choose or create the perfect spread for any question or purpose. Tarot expert and author Barbara Moore explains what makes a great tarot spread and why (including how the principles of design and psychological responses play a part), how to select a spread, how to use it once you've chosen it, and how to modify spreads or create your own. Moore presents simple techniques that will make tarot readings more fun and more accurate, and will give querents more options and control in their lives.

978-0-7387-2784-4, 264 pp., 6 x 9   **$14.95**

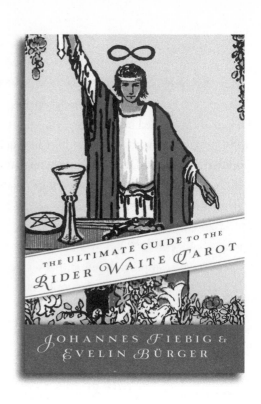

THE ULTIMATE GUIDE TO THE
RIDER WAITE TAROT

JOHANNES FIEBIG &
EVELIN BÜRGER

The Ultimate Guide to the Rider Waite Tarot
JOHANNES FIEBIG AND EVELIN BÜRGER

Originally published in Germany, *The Ultimate Guide to the Rider Waite Tarot* provides a wealth of meanings for each card of the world's most popular tarot deck. Discover the primary meaning, spiritual meaning, daily meaning, prognosis, relationship meaning, and luck meaning of each card. Authors Johannes Fiebig and Evelin Bürger also provide the ten most important symbols of each card in vibrant four-color illustrations throughout the book. In addition to an overview of the major and minor arcanas and insight into tarot's relationship with astrology, several quick top-ten lists are provided, including best tarot definitions, most important facts about tarot, favorite ways of using a single card, most useful tips for interpretation, most important rules for interpretation, and most important interpretations of each suit.

978-0-7387-3579-5, 216 pp., 6 x 9   **$18.99**

merry
meet
again

LESSONS, LIFE & LOVE ON THE PATH
OF A WICCAN HIGH PRIESTESS

DEBORAH LIPP

Merry Meet Again
Lessons, Life & Love on the Path of a Wiccan High Priestess
DEBORAH LIPP

Deborah Lipp's story is anything but ordinary. From her initiation as a third-degree Gardnerian high priestess to her marriage with celebrated Druid Isaac Bonewits to her adventures as the leader of a New York City coven, Lipp's memoir is a primer on modern Paganism and a testament to one woman's persistence and strength.

With tenderness and a true voice, Lipp describes her unique relationships with family, teachers, lovers, and friends, including icons such as Scott Cunningham and Timothy Leary. She details the ups and downs of Pagan parenting, and delves into the politics and personalities, the joys and sorrows that are found in Pagan gatherings around the world. Includes tips for practicing rituals, spells, and magic throughout.

978-0-7387-3478-1, 312 pp., 6 x 9   **$16.99**
